LA ZANDUNGA

Of fieldwork and friendship in southern Mexico

Beverly Newbold Chiñas

Prospect Heights, Illinois

For information about this book, contact:
Waveland Press, Inc.
P.O. Box 400
Prospect Heights, Illinois 60070
(847) 634-0081
www.waveland.com

Cover: The drawing, taken from Codex Borgia, represents an ancient Isthmus god "Heart of the Land"—a jaguar-god of the earth. The Aztecs used this god representation as a symbol of Tehuantepec, a name which means Hill of the Jaguar. Note that the god is seated on a hill. This hill separates Tehuantepec from San Juan and is still called Cerro del Tigre (Tiger Hill).

ISBN 0-88133-680-7

Printed in the United States of America

9 8 7 6 5 4 3

Contents

This book is dedicated to my Father and Mother
Who encouraged me and taught me about Life and the World

UNITED STATES
MEXICO
Gulf of Mexico
PACIFIC OCEAN
CENTRAL AMERICA
SOUTH AMERICA
UNITED STATES
GULF OF MEXICO
MEXICO
Mexico City
Oaxaca
Isthmus Zapotecs
CENTRAL AMERICA
PACIFIC OCEAN
0
200
400
SCALE OF MILES

PART I

Of Fieldwork and Friendship

1

First Fieldwork

Getting Ready and Getting There

As I sat at a beverage kiosk in the noon heat and looked about the El Centro plaza, my first impression was that the place was considerably larger, hotter, and dirtier than I expected. Nothing resembled the scenes in Covarrubias' *Mexico South*,* the beautiful paintings which had first captivated me and finally led me here. This was my first trip into Mexico south of Chihuahua. Two days' stopover in Oaxaca had convinced me that the capital of the state was surely one of the most primitive cities in the Western Hemisphere but now, sitting here in the heat sipping my soda, I mused how grievously I had misjudged Oaxaca. By comparison to this place, Oaxaca was a metropolitan delight.

The streets around the El Centro plaza where I now sat were dirt, the moss-stained churches observed as I entered the town all appeared to be crumbling, and the impressive turn of the century city hall in front of me was only a facade, the back part still gapingly unfinished half a century after its beginning. The church closest to the central plaza had one entire corner up through the twin bell tower split off from the main section and standing at quite a precarious angle.

"Had a recent earthquake?" I inquired of the girl attending the kiosk, pointing toward the leaning tower.

"Oh, no!" she laughed. "It's always been that way. That's the church of San Antonio. It's just old."

Determined to practice my not-too-trustworthy Spanish, I continued:

*Covarrubias, Miguel. *Mexico South: The Isthmus of Tehuantepec.* New York: Alfred A. Knopf, 1962.

"And what is that beautiful song on your radio?"

"Ay, that's 'La Zandunga.' They're playing it because it is twelve o'clock noon. They play 'La Zandunga' every day when it is twelve o'clock."

"Really! I'll remember that and set my watch by it then. It's a beautiful melody, don't you think?" I continued, trying to keep the conversation alive. "It seems familiar. I think I have heard it somewhere before."

"*Si, tal vez*. Maybe you have. 'La Zandunga' is *el son del Istmo* (regional song). Whenever you hear it, you know they are playing the music from here. When I hear 'La Zandunga,' I think of dancing at the fiestas. When I am in Oaxaca and I hear the marimbas playing 'La Zandunga,' I want to come home. 'La Zandunga' makes us *alegre*," she smiled, humming along. "But if we are far away, you know, it can also make us sad."

Having by now finished my lunch of two dwarf tacos and a cola, I paid the young lady and left to investigate a little of what was to be my new home for the next twelve months.

Traffic around the central plaza at noontime was comparable to the Los Angeles freeways at 5:15 p.m. except that the vehicles were mostly old windowless lorries, heavy farm trucks, and taxicabs. The noise from unmuffled exhausts was astounding, and the carbon monoxide fumes lent a sort of bluish cast to the dust as it rose and settled again through the churned air. Slowly circling the dusty, kiosk-cluttered *parque* (central plaza), I really wondered how and if I was going to be able to endure here for a year. Everything was so foreign, so unfamiliar; from the plants in the park to the dusky women in their long skirts and embroidered *huipiles* aggressively peddling hammocks on the street corners to the Zapotec language that ran like a murmuring river beneath the noise of traffic.

The first order of business was finding a place to stay for the night. I drove out on the highway a half mile to the only hotel listed in my guidebook. It proved to be a decaying grande dame of a hotel with beautiful tropical gardens surrounding a swimming pool verdant with algae.

The price of a room was rather steep for my modest budget, rates made possible no doubt by the hotel's exclusive guidebook listing. The dark, dank lobby with its fans turning lazily overhead and 1890s decor could have been a scene from *Casablanca*. I signed the registry for the night as a dour, haughty clerk looked on. My plan was to stay here a few days until I found some more permanent roosting spot nearer the market which was to be my first work site.

When I awoke in the night in that cramped, dingy cubicle of a room to find gigantic black cockroaches holding court in my open valise, I concluded that there *must* be something better than this overpriced roach motel and determined to locate it. A short reconnoiter next morning led me to a small family-run hotel only two blocks from the market with a sign so inconspicuous I wondered if the proprietors were trying to keep its presence a secret. As an added bonus, the reasonably clean and comfortable rooms rented for a modest sum my budget could well tolerate for a week or two. The new location would give me time to look for permanent living and working quarters while beginning research in the market.

I had chosen the Isthmus Zapotecs as the subject of my first anthropological fieldwork because theirs appeared to be a unique culture—one in which women were strong and independent, in charge of the market selling, as well as buying. Having first learned of the Isthmus Zapotecs in the library at U.C.L.A. more than a year earlier, I now had to keep reminding myself that, after months of planning, writing and rewriting the research grant proposal, I was actually here. This was it!

From the pages of *Mexico South*, Covarrubias' words still echoed in my brain. "No man, woman, or child, however humble, will acknowledge the accepted superiority of a person of another class" (299). Could they truly be so proud? Then there was his description of the women. "The frankness of Zapotec women, their rather loose use of strong language, and their social and economic independence give them a position of equality with men, and a self-reliance that is unique in Mexico" (339). With that, I was hooked.

I had been interested in women and women's status for as long as I could remember. But, as a student in anthropology, reading about women's lives in different cultures around the world was disheartening. It was always the same story, no matter what part of the world. Men did the exciting things and controlled the women, while women raised children, worked hard, and were quite powerless. Now here at last was a culture where the women were reported to be strong, assertive individuals and to have high status. I *had* to learn more about them.

The big question was: What made these women so different from all those I had been reading about in my anthropology classes?

Hundreds of other questions popped into mind. How did these women work long hours daily in the markets while caring for their families and households without the help of dishwashers, automatic clothes washers, vacuum cleaners, often even without running water or electricity? What amount and percentage of household income did Zapotec women earn and how was it spent? What were the relationships between husbands and wives? Why did some writers report that the Isthmus Zapotecs possessed a matriarchal (woman-ruled) culture while anthropologists scoffed at the idea of the very existence of matriarchy?

How did women learn their marketing skills? What part did women play in the ubiquitous fiesta system? How many children did they have and how many did they desire? Did women hold political office or vote in national elections? Did market women form unions and cooperatives? What did they want for the future and that of their children? Ultimately, it was women's economic and familial roles that were to become the focus of my doctoral dissertation research.

When colleagues learned of my plan to study the Isthmus Zapotec women, they began to share anecdotes of their travels through the area. These usually went something like this:

> Well, best of luck. I wouldn't want to tangle with those *Tehuanas*. When I passed through there last summer I tried to buy an orange from a woman in the market and she *refused* to sell it to me! She even threw a banana peel at me as I left, hitting me on the back of the head!

Or another variation on the same theme:

> Well, that should be fun! I've passed through that region several times on my way to Chiapas (or Guatemala or Central America). Those women are B-I-G mamas and look pretty mean to me. I wouldn't want to tangle with them.

This last stated by a large man as he sized up my 110 pounds.

While giving me a certain degree of pause, these tales piqued my curiosity even further. I had to discover the basis of these seemingly wild and implausible accounts of sales refusals and tossed banana skins related by persons whose integrity I trusted.

Since the artist Covarrubias' visits in the late 1930s, nothing had been published on the Isthmus Zapotecs. Nothing anthropological had been published except Frederick Starr's brief ethnography and photograph collection from his short visit of 1898. I wondered why. Once in the field, I came to wonder whether it was the reported formidability of the women or the unreported formidability of the climate that had discouraged other anthropologists from working here.

In due course the grant proposal was funded, and I set out for Mexico, a middle-aged woman driving a middle-aged pick-up truck whose canopy was packed to the roof with boxes of books, office supplies, an old typewriter, a card table and chairs, a cot, an electric fan and enough clothes and supplies to see me through the year. My son Lee, aged seventeen, was to accompany me as far as Mexico City, helping with the driving and keeping up my morale. From there, he would fly home in time for the beginning of school while I would travel the last 350 miles alone.

Alas! We had not anticipated Mexican Immigration. When we reached the checkpoint at Ciudad Juarez, we learned that no child under eighteen was allowed to enter Mexico without the signatures of *both* parents. No amount of pleading would change the Mexican authorities' minds. Lee flew back to California and I entered Mexico *solita* (alone), in the words of the immigration officer.

As I was soon to discover, Mexico is a wonderful and quixotic place, full of perplexing anomalies such as motel window screens nailed open in a mosquito-infested village and the hotel owner who refused to rent me his last room at any price because I was alone and the room was for four persons.

It did not take long to find out what that amused look on the immigration officer's face meant when I said, yes, I was traveling alone. Not many American women traveled alone in Mexico in 1966 and certainly not driving a pick-up truck! The novelty was more than most Mexican men could handle, though none was more determined than the Mexico City taxicab driver who, when I pretended not to understand Spanish, switched to fractured English long enough to ask if I did not want to "folkie, folkie."

After running the gauntlet of the best "lines" Mexican males had to offer (I still marvel at their inventiveness), I arrived in El Centro that steamy noon hour in August, 1966. Not unlike a thousand novice anthropologists before me in a thousand faraway places, I came uninvited, unannounced, and inevitably unprepared to face the challenges of fieldwork among strangers in a strange culture.

The research plan called for observing and mapping the central market during the first weeks while my language skills improved, then administering a preliminary brief questionnaire to a sizeable number of market women. This was designed to elicit enough information about my intended subjects to enable me to draw a reasonably representative sample and determine which market women I should study in more depth as a sample of the whole market entity.

My only possible contact in the Isthmus was an elderly man whom colleagues working in Oaxaca knew through the museum. He was a collector of ethnic crafts for the government-operated museums and craft stores in the state capital and a lifelong resident of the Isthmus. Hoping he might brief me on the area and introduce me to municipal officials, I went to his home early the second morning in town. He was away on a collecting trip, I was told, but expected home in three days. I left a message asking him to come to my hotel at 5:00 p.m. the following Sunday. I then spent most of the interim three days painstakingly writing out all the questions (with considerable help from a dictionary) I hoped he might answer, afraid my tongue would falter over the unfamiliar words at the critical time.

Sunday came and went without a sign of the *señor.* Then I remembered the folklore about "Mexican time." I was still operating on U.S. time while the señor would obviously be keeping "Mexican time." I expected him to show up in a day or so. When he did not, I went again to his home only to be told the same story, he was not home but would be back in three days. It seemed a futile pursuit so I set about making my own contacts wherever I could. Then one Sunday a month or so later, after I had rented and moved into a house, the old gentleman appeared at my door at the appointed hour. In my surprise and confusion, I could scarcely manage to mumble my name and ask a rudimentary question or two, having long since forgotten the whereabouts of my lengthy list of carefully prepared questions. He probably still wonders why American universities send such dim-witted persons to do field research.

Working on my own I called on the *presidente* (mayor) of the *municipio* in his office, introduced myself, presented letters of introduction from the university, and tried to explain the purpose of my stay in the area. I asked for a letter of introduction from him which I could carry about with me to explain my presence since I did not want to be mistaken for either missionary or tourist, the two categories of foreigners familiar to the local people. It was important that people know I had a legitimate reason for being in the area, asking questions, and in general just "nosing around." Otherwise, one might very well be detained by the police, something I very definitely wished to avoid. The presidente graciously obliged and I left his office with the letter in hand.

Thereafter, early in the mornings I would go to the marketplace to "hang around" for several hours, buying and sampling food items, asking questions about products, learning the layout, and letting the market women become accustomed to my presence.

The market was a dark, dank hole of a place with dirt floors; the oldest part built well over a century earlier and augmented by various jerry-built annexes over the years. Ventilation, even in this windswept Isthmus, was incredibly poor. Each morning as I stepped into the place, my nose was assaulted by the odors of rotting fruit, ripe cheese, fresh fish, and chicken guts. These were mixed with a century of garbage and grime ground into the earthen floor and blended together into an indescribable but invariably unpleasant whole. One did become accustomed to the smell after a few minutes but the first whiffs were always a trial.

Daily I appeared in the marketplace wearing a wide smile, carrying the presidente's letter of introduction tucked into my shoulder bag, and hoping to look a great deal more confident than I felt. Even though nobody asked for identification, the letter was my security blanket. After a couple of weeks I was so confident that I left the letter at home. If it had not been requested by now, I reasoned, why wear it out carrying it around? Shortly afterward I began administering the innocuous (so I thought) survey questionnaire: What is your name, age, how long have you been selling here, are you married, how many children do you have, where do you live, where were you born? The idea was to begin with simple and non-threatening questions, expecting that my continued presence might arouse people's fears and suspicions.

The plan did not work. After only a couple of days of the innocent informal questions people began asking *me* questions, which was only fair, after all. *Why did you come here? What do you want? How long are you going to stay?* I sensed their growing anxiety and asked myself what we would do at home if a citizen of Russia, India, or Japan, speaking English with a thick foreign accent, came into our businesses each day and began asking questions. Zapotec market women's reactions were no different than ours would have been in similar circumstances.

I carefully explained that I was doing my *tesis* (thesis) in order to become a teacher (an explanation which fit their knowledge of the training of teachers in Mexico and captured the spirit if not the essence of anthropological training). What seemed so incongruous to people was why an obviously rich *gringa* (after all, I was driving my own pick-up truck and could afford to rent a whole house for just one person) should come to such a "poor" place so far from home *alone* just to study their humble, broken-down old market. Some women reached the reasonable though incorrect conclusion that my story was concocted, a cover-up for some covert activity still unknown to them.

Of course I did not discover the depth of their doubts until I came in one morning to be greeted by an old woman standing on her counter-top shouting to her neighbors that they should refuse to answer anymore of the gringa's questions, that I was a spy sent by the government so that their taxes could be increased, and that nobody should cooperate in such a scheme.

Luckily, I had made a couple of friends in the market—Jonsa, a seller of beef, and her husband Leonzo, a butcher. Leonzo, in fact, had been the first person in El Centro to initiate a conversation with me on the street and to seem interested in what I was doing and offer his help. Although he did not sell in the market (virtually no men did), he came each day at noon closing time to help his wife pack up and take the unsold beef home. Jonsa and Leonzo extended their friendship and help generously in spite of the adverse publicity I was getting, becoming my first key informants and eventually my *compadres*.

For a few days after the encounter with the angry old woman, I doggedly continued coming to the market. The chilly market atmosphere progressed to freezing while I hid my sinking heart beneath the biggest smile I could muster. Most of these difficult days were spent in the refuge of Jonsa's stall learning the beef-selling business, while her neighbors glanced suspiciously at me from the corner of their eyes, wondering if I really was a spy.

The crisis was not altogether unanticipated. Such traumatic encounters are not unusual to anthropologists new in the field. But hearing about them in graduate seminars and student coffee klatches and actually facing them alone in the field are quite different experiences.

In addition to Jonsa and Leonzo, I had the good fortune to make another friend in the outdoor market annex a block away. Alberta was a jolly, thirtyish woman who sold locally-made pots. Although the spy troubles did not directly spill over into the annex, without Alberta the situation there might have become just as unpleasant.

Alberta loved to talk and had great curiosity about visitors, distant places, and languages. She relieved the monotony of her days by talking with the occasional tourist who wandered through. She was delighted when I told her I was going to be studying the markets. Alberta became my self-appointed Zapotec language teacher as we sat in her pottery stall during slack hours, I repeating the Zapotec names of all the types of pots she sold and she teaching me simple phrases. As our friendship progressed, I often brought my questions about proper responses and behavior in various situations to her. She proved to be an excellent guide to Zapotec culture and a language teacher much superior to her student.

When I tried to open a checking account in the only bank in town and was told I would have to have a local person sign the necessary form, I took the form to my new friend, Alberta, who obligingly signed it for me. Why one could not deposit money in the bank without a character reference remains a mystery to this day but I complied without protest. Confidently I returned to the bank with the signed form. The bank officer glanced over the form, reading the signature.

"Is this a local person?" he asked.

"Oh, yes, she is a native resident, she sells pots in the *plazita*," I responded.

"I am sorry, *señorita*, but you must have the signature of a *prominent* citizen of the community. This is just a market woman nobody knows."

That was my first lesson in the strength of social classes in the region. Market women were low class nobodies, while El Centro businessmen and their families, mostly non-Zapotec *mestizos*, claimed for themselves the superior status of upper class *civilisados*. The hotel owner's signature finally satisfied the banker several days later. I was too embarrassed to tell Alberta the bank would not accept her signature although, thinking back, perhaps if I had mentioned it to her she would have stormed over to the bank and demanded that they accept it. But in those early days I had yet to learn firsthand of Zapotec women's fierce pride, strong spirit, and assertive behavior.

After all the trouble, the checking account proved to be useless because nobody, not even my landlord, would accept my checks. The account's only practical function was to allow me to draw cash from the account by check.

Alberta and I later became *comadres* and to this day I owe her and Leonzo and Jonsa, my first key informants and enduring good friends deepest gratitude for the warm and unquestioning hand of friendship they extended to a stranger in the early days of fieldwork. Without them, the entire project might have collapsed early on.

Some few days after the market campaign against me was launched by the old woman, I made my usual market entry one morning to be blocked by a surly mustachioed policeman wearing a holstered pistol. He demanded, in a voice intended to intimidate, to see my "papers." Anticipating the need, I had resumed carrying the letter from the presidente of the municipio. Well, I thought, here is one problem I *am* prepared for. Smugly reaching into my bag, I whipped out the letter, opening it with what I fancied was a flourish. The man's eyes narrowed as he glanced at the letter, then with curling lip he handed it back and snarled: "This letter is completely worthless! The person who signed this letter is not the presidente. You must have a letter signed by the presidente in order to ask questions in the market."

Perplexed as I was by this unexpected news, I understood that market work was over until I could get to the bottom of the discrepancy. As I was to learn shortly, the signer of my letter was only an interim presidente placed in office by the governor of the state until the contested election had been decided. The election having been decided since my arrival, the "real" presidente was now in office.

Through Leonzo I located and rented a house only three blocks from the market and, although it was much larger than I needed and the rent was three times the amount budgeted, I signed a three-month lease. The once grand colonial mansion had seen better days, last functioning as a hospital run by missionaries several years prior to my arrival. The best features of the house were a lovely brick patio edged with lush greenery and a long screened veranda, the latter an unanticipated luxury in this land of malaria-carrying mosquitoes.

The weather was quite pleasant during these rainy season months. I made the veranda with its cool breezes into my living quarters, turned the room with the most light into an office, and ignored the rest of the house as too dark and cavernous for occupation. Although I used the office daily and repeatedly asked people to come talk with me there, not a single person ever came for an interview. It was a custom unfamiliar to local people and, as I was to learn, women did not wish to be seen entering the house of the strange gringa alone because people might gossip. A few men came alone at night, claiming to have important information, but earlier experience with too-close encounters through the marvelous inventiveness of Mexican men pursuing foreign women served me well. I refused to grant men entry, barking through the closed door: "Come back tomorrow with your wife." Of course they never did.

Leonzo was an exception, always being a perfect gentleman. He did not ask to enter the house when alone but spoke with me only in public or at the market in front of his wife. He was especially helpful to me during the first few months of fieldwork because during the day, while Jonsa was occupied at the market, he had free time to act as my guide and introduce me to various people. In his occupation as a butcher, he prepared his animals for market between 1:00 a.m. and 5:00 a.m., after which he slept until about noon. In the afternoons he took me to meet each of the thirteen *xuanas*, the prestigious and knowledgeable but politically powerless lay leaders of the barrio churches. From the xuanas I learned something about the characteristics, history, and economics of each of the thirteen barrios.

In 1966 there were very few private vehicles in the region and most men, including Leonzo, could not drive. He obviously delighted in the novelty of our visits to the xuanas with me at the wheel of the pick-up. Sometimes our routes were surprisingly circuitous as we drove up bumpy side streets and barely passable alleys so he could wave to friends. I pretended to be unaware of our roundabout routes. He had volunteered his help and I was grateful for it. Driving a few blocks out of the way was only a minor annoyance, my way of repaying him in small part for his help. Once I even unknowingly became the vehicle through which he mended a long-standing quarrel with his brother-in-law. At first puzzled by the unannounced visit to the surprised brother-in-law's home, I later learned from others that the two men had not been on speaking terms for some time prior to our visit.

Leonzo was an interested and curious informant. He knew a few words of English, and never tired of asking questions about the United States although I was never able to convince him that, yes, there are many poor people in the United States. In his mind, all North Americans were rich; the United States the proverbial land of milk and honey.

After the confrontation over the letter of introduction in the market, I thought it best to absent myself for a week or so to let things cool off. I left for a week of surveying other marketplaces of the region, a task I had fortuitously written into the original research plan. In my absence the spy story hit the front page of the weekly newspaper. I was now not just a government spy but a "Yankee imperialist spy" working for the nefarious United States government on a plot to take over the region in order to build a new inter-ocean canal. The article's author suggested that I should be deported forthwith.

Alberta showed me the spy story when I returned. I was very upset and anticipated the worst, the collapse of my whole research plan. Luck was with me, however; most of the market women were unable to read and never even saw the newspaper. After learning of the spy story, I wrote a long explanation of why I was in the area, what kinds of data I was seeking, the purposes of the questions, and the duration of my stay. I was pleased when my response was printed on the front page of the same newspaper a couple of weeks later. But if anyone read the thoughtful reply I had sweat blood over, I never learned of it. In any case, tensions eased and I was gradually able to establish rapport with most of the market women.

Beginning ethnographic research in an exotic culture is always fraught with problems. Whatever the novice anthropologist does or says in the first weeks of fieldwork will probably cause some misunderstanding or have some unintended result due to the fieldworker's inevitable naivete of the fine nuances of cultural etiquette and her inability to interpret many of the culturally prescribed cues to people's behavior. But if one is able to survive the long and lonely first months as a "strange" stranger in an exotic culture, she eventually metamorphoses from a larval graduate student—encapsulated in the cocoon of her own culture—into a professional anthropologist with a deeper sense of the value of other cultures and a new insight and appreciation of the culture she has chosen to study.

The ideal toward which the anthropologist strives is *cultural relativity*, the ability to perceive and evaluate the behavior of people in other cultures according to the rules of their culture rather than the rules of one's own. Cultural relativity comes to the anthropologist gradually over the course of the fieldwork as she gains greater knowledge and understanding of the new culture. I committed a good many social errors during my early fieldwork but mostly through sheer good fortune I was able to avoid any irretrievably disastrous consequences.

This story, *La Zandunga*, is an account, a very personal one to be sure, of fieldwork in a Zapotec peasant town in southern Mexico. Most of the book recounts experiences in 1966-67, during the first fifteen months in a pueblo with a population of about seven thousand, hereafter called San Juan. Names of places and informants have been changed to conform to anthropological ethical guidelines. The sequence of events has been rearranged in minor ways in some places to enhance the story's continuity. The last two chapters recount fieldwork experiences in San Juan after 1967, primarily the two prolonged periods spent in the field in 1975 and 1981-82.

2

Beginning

It was never my plan either to live or to work alone. As I learned so soon after entering Mexico, lone foreign women are invariably considered of questionable character, and Mexican men find them irresistible. To avoid problems, my research plan called for hiring a live-in housemaid to do the never-ending household chores. Every fieldworker in a Third World environment experiences the frustrations of trying to accomplish research while living under primitive sanitary and housekeeping conditions. At my field site, necessary tasks included sweeping floors and patios daily, marketing every morning for the day's food, preparing meals without convenience foods, doing the laundry by hand, boiling drinking water continuously for twenty minutes every other morning, and soaking vegetables and fruits in disinfecting solution before consuming them. Even for one person, housekeeping under local conditions amounted to a full-time job. A live-in housemaid could potentially become a valued informant as well.

Finding such a creature was another story. After weeks of inquiries I finally located a *vallista* (Valley of Oaxaca native) teenager who agreed to come in once a week to clean and do laundry. Once a week was better than nothing so I hired her. On her first work day the young lady appeared at my door with two siblings under age five for whom she was to care while doing her work, and a pile of family laundry to be done on my time and with my soap. A moment's reflection told me I could not afford her.

At length I located another young woman, Ana, a twenty-year-old bilingual Zapotec native of El Centro who agreed to work every other day. With Ana, I would be able to practice the elementary Zapotec I was being taught by Alberta. Ana was a steady, reliable worker when she came but as it turned out she could not come regularly. Her grandmother died and she had to observe the forty-day mourning period; she frequently failed to come when her mother was feeling poorly; she had to go to Coatzacualcos (150 miles away) on a family errand; she then contracted *la gripa* (severe chest cold); and finally she had to accompany her sister to Mexico City for surgery and was gone for an extended period. Even when she worked, I still had not solved the problem of living alone.

Another severe problem during the first months of fieldwork for the lone fieldworker is loneliness and homesickness. I relieved this to a degree by writing letters home to my two teenagers, to friends, to my mother, and to my professors. Writing letters was easy. Receiving letters from home was difficult. I never really understood why it took from two to three weeks for airmail letters to arrive from California. On very rare occasions I would receive a letter in nine days. Telephoning was too expensive except for emergencies and usually required a whole day of waiting in the long-distance office to get the call through. If the person called was not home, the entire time was wasted. If the call actually went through the connection might be so poor that it was all a waste of time and money anyway.

Leisure-time reading material was another problem. Few periodicals ordered for the purpose before I left home ever arrived. Local newsstands carried mostly adult comic books and true romances. Booksellers who set up temporary displays of more serious reading from time to time in the central plaza did not allow customers to browse through the books but insisted that the book be purchased without opening it. After a few costly gross misjudgments, I gave up trying.

About once a month, though, I would drive the 156 miles to Oaxaca for supplies (fresh fruit, cheese, peanut butter, and pickles were often on my list) where I could buy U.S. magazines and same-day Mexico City newspapers. That was a wonderful treat outranked only by the pleasure of sitting in the cool Oaxaca evenings at a sidewalk cafe eating tourist food and sipping a margarita. In Oaxaca I could speak English with American tourists, and from them learn the news from home. There was no place in the Isthmus with anything resembling a tourist (i.e., American) ambience and only rare tourists passing hurriedly through, uncomfortable in the tropical heat and dust and intent on reaching their next destination. The trips to Oaxaca were of great importance to my morale. Without them I probably could not have completed those first long months of fieldwork.

Early on I found I could brighten my lonely days by keeping fresh flowers on my work table. Truckloads of gorgeous dewy-fresh roses, gladioli, zinnias, lilies-of-the-valley, and other cool-climate varieties arrived at the central market from Oaxaca twice a week and, best of all for a poor graduate student, their cost in U.S. currency was negligible. I would purchase a bouquet daily, but each time I walked home with the bundle of flowers women I met would ask: "Who are the flowers for?" "Do you have someone in the cemetery?"

I consulted Alberta.

"Oh, people here think that flowers are just for the *los muertos* (the dead) or for the saints" was her answer.

Okay, I thought, when in the Isthmus, I will do as the Isthmenians do. I made a little household altar in the corner of my all-purpose room, where I placed a picture of Jesus, a candle, and the daily fresh flowers. Thereafter when asked about the flowers, I replied, "For my *santa mesa*" (household shrine). Ana no doubt told her family and friends about my new shrine and the word got around that the gringa was not an *evangelista* (Protestant missionary).

In addition to a live-in housekeeper, I had been searching for a literate research assistant who could act as a translator of Zapotec and could run interference for me with the various officials and other men from whom I needed information. Finding a young person who was literate in Spanish, a native speaker of Zapotec, and who had time to spare proved impossible. Anyone literate was either fully employed, working in another city, or enrolled in classes full time.

One day Leonzo brought me Alfredo, the high school English teacher, who volunteered to help, mistakenly believing I was an archaeologist. Alas, everyone loves archaeology. When he learned that my research had to do with live people, perhaps families of some of his students, his enthusiasm cooled. Since he was not native to the Isthmus and did not speak Zapotec, his utility to the project was marginal anyway. Thus, after doing a survey of the business establishments in El Centro he left for summer vacation and our association terminated. The plan of hiring a helper-translator seemed doomed.

By sheer good fortune, I had arrived in the Isthmus during the most agreeable weather of the entire year, the rainy season. For the first few weeks the rains had been brief torrential downpours that left the air sparkling if oppressive with humidity. I was working in the market again, the spy story now history, and a number of women were graciously cooperating. Then the rainy season abruptly ended.

Within days, as I trudged to the market each morning all was dust—powdery, coppery dust. The infamous north wind, locally known as *El Norte*, became more and more insistent each day and often continued its gusty roar nonstop for several days and nights. The shutters banging, the wind moaning through the old house's crevices and ventholes, and the dust and sand sifting relentlessly through everything began to grate on my nerves. Nearly every day when I returned from the market, dust would be so thick on the table that the pattern of the oilcloth had disappeared. With only a few weeks remaining on my lease, I determined to find another place away from El Centro and the now-dry riverbed from which much of the blowing sand came. I thought a smaller community where I might integrate more easily into the daily life, truly get to know women and their families on their home ground rather than at their place of business, would be more advantageous for the next phase of the project.

Again I enlisted the help of Leonzo who suggested a modern-style house in their neighborhood of nearby San Juan. I had noticed the house from the highway far across the river when I first arrived, although at the time I did not know it was vacant or to whom it belonged. The house stood out from afar because it was different from all the other houses and sat on a high rock outcrop overlooking the river. From that distant vantage point, the house appeared huge and incongruous with its uncharacteristic crackerbox shape, flat roof, rows of windows, and moss-stained whitewash. Later I learned that the opposite end of the house hung sentinel-like over a narrow passageway chiseled through the rock, marking the entrance to San Juan.

Tiu Tono, the owner, was already known to me through Leonzo. I had interviewed him several times about "the old days." Eighty-one years old, Tiu Tono was afflicted with a grave throat ailment and bouts of an astonishing edema which periodically caused his frail legs to blacken and swell to elephantine proportions. In his gruff way he seemed pleased to share his knowledge of the past and the pueblo with me although he was rather inclined to wander off the subject of history into his own health problems. Still, I sensed that he rather enjoyed my visits and guessed that he might rent the house to me. At dusk one evening I made my way out to his house.

Greeting him with the appropriate "*Buenas noches*, Tiu Tono," I climbed up the several steep steps from the street to where he sat in his usual spot, just inside his entrance, facing the street. His chair was directly in front of a dust-laden, ancient ice cream cabinet. A faded *Paletaria* sign hung outside, though now at a rakish angle. It was apparent that no *paletas* (popsicles) had been sold here for some time. He indicated the other chair, saying he was "keeping the store" for Rufina who was out back tending her chickens. Tiu Tono and Rufina, his middle-aged spinster daughter, lived here in squalor in one room and the *corredor* (veranda) behind the "store," which consisted of a counter placed at right angles to the ice cream cabinet. From this counter Rufina occasionally sold a liter of kerosene, a bar of soap, or some matches to a neighborhood child.

Folks said that Tiu Tono was wealthy, but there was little in his home or business to support such a rumor. True, he owned some valuable property close to the pueblo, but I suspected that his one-time small fortune, like Tiu himself, was on the brink of collapse.

I approached the subject, a place to live for the next nine months. In his gravelly old man's voice, Tiu croaked that he had never considered renting the house because children annoyed him and who else but a family with several children would rent such a large house? Since I was alone he would consider it. He rapped his cane against the counter, bringing Rufina running, and asked her to take me up the hill to look at the empty house. It had been several years since he had been able to climb the hill, he explained, but Rufina went up daily to water the small fenced garden. It was a moonless night, but Rufina thought a light on the corredor still functioned. We went out into the dark well of Tiu's backyard, groping our way up the hill. I could just make out two gaping caverns under the left half of the house. In the darkness, these openings gave the effect of a double garage without doors.

Rufina opened a makeshift gate which she had set up to keep the chickens out of the garden. The light bulb flickered in response to Rufina's hand on the switch, and miraculously, though dimly, remained on. Bats flitted about the edges of night, startled at the disturbance.

We peered into the main room, whose door lay on the floor as if it had fallen off its hinges. I could see that the door and floor were covered with inches of dirt and debris. I wondered if the house would be habitable. Rufina explained that the house had never been finished. Door casings were missing, only a few of the lights worked, there was no water and no drain in the room intended to serve as a kitchen although a sink was evident in the corner, a decidedly urbane feature.

Like many Mexican houses, there were no closets, no counters, and no shelves. The bathroom had a toilet and showerhead. The only deficiencies here seemed to be water and a missing section of drainpipe beneath the lavatory. Someone had bridged that gap by bending a piece of tin into a chute and propping it up under the sink to run the water onto the floor and from there into a central floor drain.

The house was ten years old but looked forty, constructed for—but never occupied by—Tiu's only son, an accountant who lived in Mexico City with his city-bred wife and several children. Neighbors later told me the daughter-in-law had flatly refused to live in San Juan but the family came once in a while for a few days' visit. Although many window panes were cracked or missing, a house with windows, so atypical of the region, seemed bright and cheerful to me, even in the dingy gloom of night. I decided it was worth a try.

In back of Tiu's house at the bottom of the hill was the entrance from the street—just wide enough to accommodate an oxcart. I agreed to take the house if I could get my pick-up through the entrance. Vandals had already broken off the mirror and committed other damage during the months the vehicle was parked in front of my other house. I thought more months on the public street would see it completely cannibalized.

Early the next morning, I attempted to negotiate the entrance. With only about three inches to spare on either side of the entrance gate, it took some fine maneuvering from the narrow rock-walled street but I managed to get the truck through the gate without a scratch. We signed a six-month lease.

When I mentioned my impending move to San Juan, the hotel owner and the few other mestizo business people in El Centro I had come to know were, without exception, aghast.

"But, señorita, you can't live in San Juan! A woman alone in San Juan? Impossible! You must find another place."

Author's field office and living quarters

When they perceived my determination, they countered with: "You must find someone to live with you! You must buy a pistol!"

Alarmists, I thought, and hired Ana for a few consecutive days to help clean my new abode. The first piece of equipment needed was a shovel. I borrowed one from Tiu Tono. We shoveled steadily, cleaning out the years of dirt and debris accumulated on the floors of the doorless rooms. I now understood clearly for the first time how archaeological ruins become buried. A few more years of neglect and this house too would have been buried under a mound of sand.

Our first sweeps with the shovel rewarded us with a treasure, tiled floors. I was just as pleased to find that the ugly flat roof was surrounded by a low wall and accessible by an outside staircase. From the roof I could survey the countryside far up the river valley and into the mountains to the northwest and out over the coastal plain almost to the sea in the opposite direction. I could also observe everyone who passed the house on either side, along the river path or through the narrow entrance to the pueblo. At sunrise and sunset the roof was to become my favorite spot as I watched the magnificent sunsets and the people of San Juan, still mostly strangers to me, coming and going below.

The next step in the house reclamation project was to hire a handyman to rehang the doors, replace broken windowpanes, connect plumbing and rig up a water supply, then repair the faulty electrical connections, all at my expense but justified by the low rent I would pay. I had some misgivings about the vulnerability of the house to intruders (the seed had been planted by El Centro acquaintances) with so many barless, screenless windows, but Tiu Tono assured me it was perfectly safe. Who could scale the twenty-foot sheer rock wall from the street? (It turned out that somebody could, but more about that later). Just to reassure me, he ordered a couple of boys to cut some thorny bushes and lay the brush around the ledge under my windows on the street side.

I promised myself that I would definitely find someone to stay with me, even if only a boy or an old man to sleep on the corredor at night and act as *velador* (night watchman). Tiu Tono persuaded a fourteen-year-old grandnephew to come over at dark the first few nights to "guard the gringa." The boy came but insisted on sleeping locked in one of the rooms. I had to ask myself who was guarding whom. After a few nights he did not show up at all. Much later I learned that he and everyone else in San Juan were afraid of the dozens of bats that roosted during the day under the cavernous unfinished end of the house and spent their nights sweeping across the corredor in search of moths. I was not crazy about bats myself but spent many nights sleeping there anyway, cocooned in my hammock, taking advantage of the evening breeze. I continued to live alone.

While I was working daily in the El Centro market, feeding myself was not much of a problem. I could order a hot meal there and buy whatever I needed daily. But after moving to San Juan buying and preparing food each day required much more time than I was willing to spend. The San Juan market was very small and limited in offerings and a shopping trip to El Centro required more than an hour each morning. Things had to be simplified, and I ultimately ended up living most of the time on hard cheese, dried shrimp, and *totopos* (cracker-like tortillas) plus the peanut butter and powdered milk I brought from

Oaxaca. None of these foods required refrigeration or preparation, making them both available any time and quick to prepare. Along with an orange, mango, or other fruit which could be purchased on the street near my house, this was a fairly adequate and satisfying diet.

I soon found I could order a hot dish once a week from my neighbor Tivi, who prepared foods in quantity for the Sunday market. Her most frequent dish was iguana in *mole* (a spicy red sauce). In season she sold quail, venison, rabbit, armadillo, and other game in mole. When no game was available she prepared chicken or turkey in the same sauce. Although it was not my favorite, I frequently had iguana, a famous regional dish. Tasting similar to chicken, iguana was not unpalatable but the numerous little bones and black, scaly skin rather put me off. I much preferred the armadillo but it was not often available. Tivi teased me about my preference, jokingly calling me Bevi *Ngupi* (armadillo). Comadre Jonsa often sent over a small piece of liver, *cecina* (dried beef), or fruit. All in all, I found I could make out quite well without daily food shopping.

Ice and fresh green leafy vegetables were the items I missed most. Ice was available by the chunk but was not made from purified water and was left sitting on the sidewalk in the dirt when delivered. I could use it to cool bottled beverages and fruits but could not have lemonade, iced tea, or water with ice in it.

Before I was really settled in Tiu Tono's house, it was December and getting drier and windier each day. I fell into a state of anxious depression, well-known to anthropologists at this juncture in fieldwork. I had been here some four months and what did I have to show for it? I began to lie awake nights, to brood, to have doubts about whether I would be able to complete the project.

In retrospect, I had accomplished a good deal, but at the time it all seemed like nothing. Tasks completed included mapping most of the two marketplaces in El Centro, with their more than 360 individual sellers, talking with local officials, and ferreting out and recording a respectable amount of local history and background information. I had good, helpful friends and informants in Leonzo and Jonsa and Alberta. I had attended more fiestas than I would have preferred (they were all much alike in structure), and I had learned a fair amount of general details about the culture. Still, I fretted. What should be my next move? Research plans and research schedules probably never pan out in the field as they are planned from a faraway university months in advance, but my state of mind was such that all I perceived was failure. There were so many tasks still to accomplish but how was I to go about it?

I had come to study the women—these women who were constantly scuttling through the streets barefoot, their long, full skirts trailing in the dust. Most carried enormous loads atop their heads, hurrying here and there, selling and buying. I wanted to know more about them—what they thought, what they liked and disliked about their lives, what kinds of activities they enjoyed, how much money they earned, how they spent it, and so much more. Did they often quarrel with their husbands and about what, how often did they go to fiestas (I already knew it was their major entertainment), what did they talk about among themselves? Except for the market contacts I had made, the women seemed so unapproachable. The homes of Leonzo and Jonsa and of Alberta, who lived across the river, were the only Zapotec homes to which I had been invited as an individual guest rather than as one of many fiesta attendants. When I carried a camera in the streets, women covered their faces. When I walked in unfamiliar parts of town, naked little boys scurried away a block in advance, crying "*Ñaa, Ñaa*, the Gringa!" more frightened than if they had seen a ghost. Seeing a ghost after all was not so rare in Zapotec life as seeing a *dxu* (foreigner).

I had moved to San Juan to make friends with village women, many of whom sold only irregularly in the markets where they had no permanent places but moved around or sat on the floor or sidewalk with their wares. I had learned a little about the region's social classes during my days studying the markets, beginning with the checking account incident. The market sellers and most of their customers considered themselves to belong to two distinct social classes, *humilde* (lower) and *de cultura* (upper). The market and village Zapotec women were placed in the subordinate position, while the mestizo "city" women were considered high class with their self-defined status as "civilisadas." Where were those proud Zapotec women of whom Covarrubias wrote? Being an American and living in El Centro had automatically placed me in the upper class in people's minds and hampered my attempts at rapport with village women. How was I to counteract this disadvantage?

As Christmas neared there was no denying it, I was depressed and intensely homesick. Mail from California remained as unreliable as ever. A letter from home rarely arrived in less than two weeks and often took three weeks or more. Eventually I was to find that a good deal of mail simply never arrived. But not knowing that, I worried because I did not hear from my children often enough and letters from others were even more infrequent.

I made the three-hundred mile round trip to the state capital in early December to boost my morale and to do some archival research. While there I located and brought home a ratty-looking plastic Christmas tree about two feet high and a few brightly painted tin ornaments. The tree, when set up in the corner of my office-living room, was more depressing than the empty space it filled. Christmas in the Isthmus, despite the poetic quality of the phrase, is culturally about as alien to the North American variety as is possible to imagine. First, it was not then marked by major commercial efforts at promotion, while the ambience of Zapotec culture and the distinctly tropical weather made the holiday seem decidedly unlike Christmas. There were special street markets between December 25 and January 6 (the day some small gifts are given to children) and a few small neighborhood *posadas*, consisting of a procession of children carrying the image of infant Jesus from house to house and to the churches, but even with these events I could not work up any Christmas spirit. I missed my children and the whole holiday spirit which pervades December at home. Since parcel post from the United States never reached its Mexican destination in those days, I had told family and friends before I left not to send any packages, a decision I now regretted deeply. Just knowing something had been sent but did not arrive would have been preferable to not expecting anything. Then the day before Christmas I fell ill with the worst case of gastroenteritis I was to suffer during the entire year.

3

Questions, Questions

Not far into the project I noticed that people hesitated to speak freely whenever I tried to take notes on the spot. In view of this reluctance, tape-recording was out of the question too. In light of the general distrust of note-taking and the spy brouhaha, I tried to ask questions in an innocuous, offhand manner. People were used to communicating orally and were at ease with casual conversation, which became a major mode of operation for me as well. At midday break and in the evenings I made notes at home on what I had learned that day. With a little practice, I could recall conversations I needed to remember almost word-for-word for several hours.

I knew at some point I had to get back to a more structured gathering of data for some aspects of the project in order to have a quantified basis for some of the conclusions I would eventually reach about women's economic roles and the community in general. But much of an anthropologist's data, and I think the most culturally revealing, is unquantifiable. How does one quantify the nuances of language or the subtle ways in which people convey messages non-verbally? How does one quantify women's solidarity, or women's power? What data were quantifiable—vital statistics, household inventories, school enrollments, and market transactions, for example—needed to be collected in a systematic way.

The first two pieces of information a fieldworker needs are a map of the community and an idea of how many people live there. The map, even a crude one the worker draws by walking the bounds of the pueblo, will define the limits of the community, make finite and explicit the territory of that place which is being studied. A census, even a rough one made from counting houses, will give some idea of the size of the population from which one will draw some dozens of informants and, with luck, from one to five or more key informants.

Key informants are the ethnographer's right-hand helpers, local individuals who are interested in the research, insightful into their own culture, and yet have the ability to see beyond their culture, to envision it from afar to some degree, much as the ethnographer does. Key informants are almost invariably highly intelligent individuals, curious about the world around them. Sometimes they are the first to come forward to offer friendship and aid to the anthropologist as was the case with Leonzo, or one may stumble onto a key informant quite by chance. Key informants must be willing and able to spend countless hours answering questions and explaining aspects of the culture as requested by the fieldworker. Many people do not have the time or patience to be key informants. Key informants provide the continuity and long-term, in-depth data an anthropologist needs to understand the culture, working with the researcher steadily for long periods, often throughout the entire field project. The closest relationships between the anthropologist and the people are those formed with key informants who also regularly become the anthropologist's lifelong friends. Leonzo, Jonsa, and Alberta were my first three key informants, although Jonsa did it more as a favor to her husband than because she enjoyed the role. Good fortune would bring me several others over the next months and into the next two decades.

Of the two pieces of information I first needed, a census and a map, the map was the easiest to acquire. In 1967, the presidente of San Juan had some copies of a hand-drawn pueblo map with the names of all the streets and alleys which, although not drawn to scale, served my purpose admirably. (When I requested a new map in 1990 to acquaint me with the many new streets and alleys, I was dismayed to find that it was the same map I had been given over twenty years earlier.)

The census was another matter. When I first moved to San Juan, in answer to my inquiry about how many people lived in the pueblo, Leonzo mentioned that his son was taking part in a school census. Sixth-graders were surveying the entire community house-by-house, collecting names, gender, ages, and level of education of every resident, as well as occupations of household heads. This census was important to the pueblo and to the schools because the national government based its financial support on such census figures. What a stroke of luck if I could get a copy of it! It would not only save me days, even weeks, of toil collecting even a partial census, it would provide the names, addresses, and ages of all the residents from which I could select a reasonable (although not random) sample of families from whom I might collect detailed household statistics.

Colleagues working in Oaxaca had generously provided me with a six-page household questionnaire they were using in similar studies in the Valley of Oaxaca. I thought I knew enough about Isthmus Zapotec culture by now to begin revising some of the questions to suit Isthmus conditions and culture. If I asked essentially the same questions, rephrased to be appropriate to the local conditions, we would have data from two different ecological zones and two different cultures to use comparatively. The first step was to get some sort of a census from which a sample could be drawn. The next step would be to have the questionnaire translated from Spanish to Isthmus Zapotec, and then the most difficult part, to gain the cooperation of a sample of some fifty families to answer the questions. This household questionnaire was to form the core of the whole project, although the data I wanted to collect would ultimately go far beyond its limitations.

Coming to my rescue again, Leonzo introduced me to the teacher who was in charge of the census. No, the teacher said, he no longer had a copy; he had turned it over to his superior in El Centro. I traced down his superior and found he too had already passed it on to *his* superiors at the regional office twenty miles away. He thought a copy was floating around the community somewhere, and suggested I talk to the presidente of the *ex-distrito* (a political division made up of several municipios) whose office was in El Centro. Repeated attempts to lay hands on a copy of that census consumed far too many days of my time with visit after visit to the ex-distrito secretary who always courteously promised to help but never did. I suspected I was getting the royal runaround and gave up the chase, though not the mission.

Disappointed, I moved ahead with my own informal house count, just walking along the streets methodically counting entrances to *solares* (the enclosed lot and dwelling) with a hand-held counter.

Although not 100 percent reliable (sometimes there are two or three families who use the same entrance), such a count would give me a ballpark figure of the population. This was a task I could do without help in the cooler early morning hours. The only problem was that when I walked alone in unfamiliar neighborhoods, every woman I met inquired where I was going. Later I understood that this was just a Zapotec greeting similar to our "How do you do?" They did not expect an answer but I did not know that at the time. I thought telling them I was counting houses was apt to end in another spy scare. I imagined their reaction would be: 'Yes, she *is* working for the government and they want to collect taxes on our houses, that's why she is counting them.' (I learned much later that from their viewpoint that would be a reasonable assumption since most people only paid their real estate taxes if compelled to in order to sell the property). I began carrying an old pair of sandals with me and when asked I replied I was on my way to the shoe repairman. (There was one in every part of town). That was not a complete fabrication. With all the walking I was doing and the rough terrain, I did have shoes to repair frequently.

Women I met on the street in San Juan were usually not unfriendly although little children were frequently frightened of me. (This is not surprising since their mothers were telling them that the gringa would come and steal them away if did not behave.)

I soon noticed that old women sitting in doorways were always looking out for me even though we had never met. When I walked near the edge of town where fields join the last houses, inevitably an old woman would beckon me from her doorway.

"Pssssst, psssst. Don't go out in the fields. It is not safe," she would say in hushed tones.

Sometimes I would be walking along in the center of town when I would hear that familiar "psssst, psssst" and women would wave me into their doorway.

"Wait here until that *borracho* (drunk) has passed," they would whisper. I had not even noticed the weaving figure approaching half a block away.

I appreciated their concern and discovered that it was just one of many manifestations of Zapotec women's esprit de corps. Even though I was a stranger, they assumed I needed the same protection and guidance they gave their own daughters. I basked in this feeling of comradery and gender unity which was so different from what I had ever experienced in my own culture. In San Juan I never had to worry about men making coarse suggestions to me. (Mestizos in El Centro were another matter.) I thought about the reason. Maybe, I thought, it is because Zapotec men have more respect for women than mestizo men do. Certainly they behave more decorously while sober and in their own pueblo. Eventually I came to understand that Zapotec women's power lies, in no small part, in the moral support and protection they give one another and this in turn influences men's behavior toward them.

With the household questionnaire, I could no longer make do without a helper, a native speaker of Zapotec who could translate the questions to Zapotec and then ask the questions in ways understandable to local folks. Leonzo suggested a young mother who had recently received her teaching credential and was waiting for a job opening. Betina had grown up in San Juan—raised by her Zapotec grandmother— and then moved to the city to earn her teaching credential. She and her husband, also a teacher and San Juan native, had served their teaching internship in a tiny, isolated village high in the mountains where part of their training required that they write an ethnography of the community. Through her own experience with their ethnographic research, she easily identified with my work in San Juan.

Betina was about twenty-five years old, pretty and plump, always jolly and telling jokes and stories. Her gregariousness and good nature made her an ideal candidate for an interviewer. The catch was that she had two small daughters, ages one and three, and, having just recently returned to the pueblo, the family was renting a cramped, earth-floored house without running water or electricity. Her family and household duties occupied most of her time. But she agreed to help me translate the questionnaire to Zapotec and, with some persuasion, to help interview people whenever she could get away.

In the late afternoons when her husband had gone back to school after the midday break, she translated the many questions one-by-one while I wrote them down in phonetic Zapotec. That done, I had another problem—how to get approximately sixty copies of the translated questionnaire reproduced. There were no copy machines in the entire Isthmus at the time. I had to type the six legal-length pages on the old-fashioned blue gelatin stencils and take these to the university in Oaxaca to get them run off. All this took more than a week.

In January the north wind vents its full fury on San Juan, while temperatures begin increasing. My house, perched high on its rock outcrop, caught every gust. Windows rattled and curtains billowed like opening parachutes (I had cut up sheets to make the curtains). With frustrating regularity, the wind ripped the curtains from their makeshift hangers and flung them angrily to the dust-covered floor. Houses in San Juan had few windows, none of them curtained. I began to understand why. One particularly gusty night the wind actually tore the top sheet off me as I lay sleeping, waking me with a start. Closing the windows had little effect. By now more panes were missing than in place and rocks propelled by little boys' slingshots continued to take their toll.

The dust, heat, and wind greatly depressed me. There seemed to be no escape. In the streets the coarse gravel nipped sharply at one's ankles and the blowing sand gnawed at one's eyes. Women hurried through the streets holding their *rebozos* over their faces, their long dark skirts flapping incessantly around their ankles. They bent low into the wind and carried their baskets on their arms rather than atop their heads as they had during rainy season.

During these hot, windy January days, Betina and I, with her two tots in tow, began administering the questionnaire to Betina's relatives, comadres, and neighbors. If we stuck strictly to business, each questionnaire required more than an hour. But Betina was too extroverted and fun-loving to hold so closely to the task and, like everyone but me, she was not much concerned with time. We only occasionally completed two questionnaires in an afternoon.

The questions, directed to the woman of the house, included: Do you have a radio? How many hammocks do you own? What pieces of gold jewelry do you own? From whom do you borrow emergency money? Then there were questions about income-producing activities of each adult, occupations, land owned, land rented, animals owned, level of schooling of each member, ages and birth dates of each person, how many compadres had they and who they were, and how often had they attended fiestas during the recent past. I hoped to gain some idea of relative wealth and status differences between households which might provide clues about social status, what share of household income was earned by women, how women spent household income, and what they thought was important to their future and their children's future.

By pre-testing the questionnaire in a couple of households, we learned that some of the questions dealt with locally sensitive subjects—the amount of land owned, the amount of land farmed, amount of property taxes paid, recent improvements to homes, and numbers of animals owned. Long experience with government bureaucracy had taught people that questions such as these might result in increased pressure to pay taxes. In addition, I soon found that land ownership and quantity were the most sensitive subjects in the entire pueblo. This was partly because the municipio, communally owning most of the land, was continuously involved in lawsuits with neighboring municipios over boundaries and partly because everyone knew of cases where people had lost their private land holdings through sly, unscrupulous legal maneuvers by outsiders. People refused to discuss land, would not even disclose prices of land recently bought or sold, and certainly would never tell an outsider such as I how much land they owned. Although modest on the subject of sexual behavior, they might have been more willing to discuss this semi-taboo subject than land.

To allow us to collect as much information as possible before the sensitive subject of land came up, after the pretest we deferred all sensitive questions to the end of the interview. If the interviewee decided to terminate the interview, we still had vital statistics and other pertinent but less sensitive data on the household. Everyone was told at the beginning they were free to end the interview at any time without rancor on our part. Once I learned how sensitive land questions were, most of these were stricken from the format. I would have to find some other approach to gathering information about land. After we had rearranged the questions, almost everyone cooperated fully.

Finding the right time to interview people—so that it did not interfere with their own tasks—was somewhat of a challenge. People preferred interviews between 1:00 and 4:00 p.m., the *siesta* hours when women were almost always home resting or engaged in quiet tasks. These were also the most intensely hot hours of the day. Looking back, I marvel at Betina's patient cheerfulness and willingness to help.

Because of the heat and missed naps, the toddlers became bored and tired. After a couple of disruptive episodes of crying, I offered to pay Betina's neighbor to keep the children for a couple of hours while we interviewed. This worked well for two days, until Betina decided she could not leave them because her departure caused the babies to cry. We continued to take the poor tykes with us. I was to learn gradually over the months that Zapotec parents are very concerned with not making small children sad because it is thought that children can die of *tristeza* (sadness). Since many small children do sicken and die (and sick children often appear to be sad), no parent wants to take the risk of making a child sad.

Experience soon taught me that the anthropologist's project has to fit in with people's ongoing lives. In the Isthmus, scheduling and carrying anything out was extremely complicated due to the endless succession of fiestas, weddings, funerals, mourning periods, illnesses, and other events which make up the fabric of Zapotec life. Too many wasted days at the beginning of fieldwork when some planned interview or task had to be postponed because of an informant's changes in schedule—an emergency trip to another city, an illness in the family, or attendance at a fiesta—led me to begin scheduling several alternative tasks for each day. If the first fell through, the time could be devoted to another fruitful research task. If all else failed, there were always stacks of field notes to type and the informal house count I was still working on.

The interviewing with Betina dragged on at a snail's pace. Betina's daughters were ill several times, then her grandfather died and she could not work for the traditional forty-day mourning period. Several times she had to take days off to travel to the state capital to try to find out why her husband's paychecks had not arrived. Another "fly in the soup" of which I was only belatedly informed was that Betina's husband had become involved in some sort of bitter political dispute. This came to light one day when Betina remarked that she did not like to walk past the office of the presidente, who I then learned was the leader of the opposing side of the conflict. There were a few families who hereafter always identified me with the wrong side of that conflict, about which I knew nothing, simply because of my association with Betina.

In spite of all the handicaps and delays, Betina and I were eventually able to complete twenty-seven interviews, exhausting her wide circle of cooperating families. I began to look for another helper in a distant part of the pueblo in order to widen the base of sample families.

Roberto, a young man who had converted to Jehovah's Witnesses, had introduced himself soon after I moved to San Juan. A potter by trade, he was the leader of the new group of Jehovah's Witness converts, all of whom were potter families. He spoke a little English and was trying to learn more which he needed in order to communicate with his church superiors in the city. He first sought me out because he thought I might be a Protestant missionary.

Roberto seemed quite knowledgeable about his culture and his end of the pueblo and it was a chance for me to collect household data from the people he represented, his relatives and the handful of other potter families in his section of the pueblo. He agreed to help me with some questionnaires in exchange for a few hours of tutoring in English but I had to agree not to take snapshots in his section of the pueblo, something his new religion forbade.

Roberto was a reed-thin individual with a face to match and an aquiline nose which gave him a visage resembling the kingly personages carved on a Mayan stele. From Leonzo I learned that the potters were a group apart from the rest of the pueblo, having moved from Xochitlan (twenty miles away) a couple of generations previously. In San Juan, as long as anyone remembers that your ancestors came from somewhere else, you will always be something of an outsider, even if they came from a community only twenty miles away eighty years earlier.

The potter families were mostly landless, dependent on their pottery production for income. In 1967, plastic and metal containers were becoming common and pottery was rising in price as wood to fire the kilns became scarce and expensive. The potters were having a difficult time making a living. They were also economically unable to participate more than peripherally in the fiesta system, and these may have been primary reasons for their religious conversion. As Jehovah's Witnesses, they rejected belief in the saints and the Catholic-based festivals, and scorned drinking alcohol. Tobacco use, coffee, and tea were also forbidden. The townspeople still purchased their pottery from them although competition from nearby Xochitlan was fierce. Whatever the reason, Roberto had convinced all the potter families to convert and was also introducing sanitary ways of handling food and water and a new way to make a living—manufacturing cement blocks.

Roberto's one shortcoming, from my viewpoint, was that he was given to preaching his new religion to me at every opportunity and it sometimes required a bit of creative thought on my part to get him off the subject and back to research topics. Roberto and I completed about a dozen questionnaires among his relatives and neighbors and I received the added bonus of getting to know a different segment of the community. I was able to learn something of the economics of pottery making, as well as watching the potters work. The ban on picture taking was a price I had to pay. To this day I have never been able to get any pictures of the potter families or of the potters at work making their huge jars, each almost as tall as a man, coiling the clay around and around and pressing it in place with their hands to form a perfectly symmetrical vessel, all without the use of a potter's wheel.

By the time Roberto and I finished our group of questionnaires, I had heard the questions asked in Zapotec so often that I felt I could administer the remaining questionnaires myself with the help of a native speaker to make contacts and to translate the Zapotec answers for me as needed. This meant that I no longer needed a literate individual as a helper and opened the field of possible helpers much wider. I still needed between ten and fifteen completed questionnaires. Who would I find to help me? A first requirement was someone not related to either Betina or Roberto so that we would again have a different segment of the population in our sample. For once a request for suggestions from Leonzo was not immediately productive, but I still had several months to complete the remainder of the questionnaires. Until I found another helper, I could pursue several other avenues of research.

One of these avenues was an investigation of the *viajeras*, women who travel around to other markets, sometimes as far as five hundred miles away, to sell their products. Almost since my arrival in the field I had been inquiring about the viajeras; who they were and where I could contact some of them. The sister of my comadre Alberta was a viajera and Alberta spent months working on getting the two of us together. With luck, she would be willing to let me travel with her on one or more of her junkets. But she, like all viajeras, was hard to catch. Usually these women are only home a couple of days to restock their merchandise and then are off again on another journey lasting between three days and three weeks. Their schedules are not regular so it is sheer luck to find a viajera at home.

A second research vein I was exploring was the possibility of gaining access to the municipio records of births and deaths. The household surveys indicated that there was a high infant mortality rate. Nearly every family had lost at least one child somewhere between birth and age three. Many had lost two, and three was not uncommon. An examination of the municipio records could give me a more precise idea of the percentages and causes of the infant deaths. An inquiry to the local doctor confirmed what I had suspected, that many infant deaths were due to impure water and resulting gastroenteritis.

If I were to get a chance to see the municipio records I also wanted to check the causes of deaths for adults. There was a seemingly high rate of diabetes and I heard disturbing reports of adults dying of tetanus and rabies—two serious hazards to life easily preventable by inoculations of people and animals. Then there were the homicides, several of which had occurred since my arrival. The victims were all men, mostly young, seemingly the end results of the feuds and political disputes which appeared to be endemic to the community.

The third research area which intrigued me was land. Since I was blocked by cultural sensitivity from directly asking questions about land, I looked for other ways to gain information. Sometimes I overheard family members commenting on the price of a piece of land that had been sold. I asked at the Irrigation District office about the total land area of the municipio of San Juan and was given a suspiciously round figure. I later determined that this was only an estimate due to the fact that Irrigation District officials had been unable to survey San Juan land because of strong citizen resistance. A request by Leonzo that I drive a group of men to one of the outlying *colonias* to get a hidden land map to present in court gave me a rare opportunity to openly discuss land disputes in a non-threatening way. By such informal and fortuitous circumstances, I gradually collected a good deal of information about land over the months.

I spent slack periods of time working on ways to get into the municipio records and to actually contact and get acquainted with some viajeras. The municipio records proved to be the most difficult.

What is so complicated about looking at the municipio records? Unlike in the United States, one cannot just go to the city hall and ask for them. In San Juan as in most of Mexico, one needs *palancas* in order to get information, get a job, ask a favor of a casual acquaintance, negotiate a disputed electricity bill with the power company—in short, to accomplish much of anything.

The *palanca* (literally translated as a crowbar or a lever) is someone who will act as an intermediary on one's behalf in dealing with a third party. Palancas are usually relatives or compadres to persons on both sides of the desired transaction. In other words, I would ask someone who is obligated to me or a relative or compadre to intervene on my behalf with a compadre, relative, employer, or in-law of his from whom I want something. The blank walls I encountered in the local bureaucracy during the first months of fieldwork were probably largely due to my lack of palancas. People without palancas, strangers such as I, might sometimes gain favors and information through bribery but this is a minefield fraught with danger since it is illegal and could conceivably lead to one's arrest if offered to the wrong person. I thought it prudent to steer clear of any hints of offering bribes.

As I learned the system and gained more friends and several compadres, I too was able to make use of palancas. Success lay in seeking out people to intervene to whom the third party would find it difficult to say no.

I had not found the right palanca with the school census and I did not want to risk the same fate with the municipio records. I would continue to ask around, and persevere until the person or persons who could act as palancas to the municipio records surfaced.

In addition to perseverance, flexibility proved to be a valuable asset—a means to avoid wasted days when a planned interview or engagement was cancelled. As I became acquainted with people through the questionnaire interviews, visiting elders whose health might prevent them from getting out was a very productive and mutually enjoyable alternative activity. Typing pages of hastily pencilled notes was a last resort standby, and the one least enjoyed, when all else failed.

4

La Zandunga

One morning at the beginning of February, I stepped out of my doorway on a house-counting mission to discover it was the fiesta day of San Juan's very own patron saint. Although I was aware that the fiesta was coming and preparations had been in progress for weeks, I had completely lost count of the days. Fiestas were not a major research interest, consuming as they did big blocks of time away from collecting data on the topics of my project—markets and women.

On this morning I found the streets around my neighborhood filled with people in their fiesta costumes, crowding into the church courtyard across the street. Firecrackers and music began to punctuate the morning air. I hurried back up to my house for a camera and spent the morning taking pictures of the processions and crowds as they gathered at the church. Fiesta times were then the only occasions when people welcomed photographers. At these festive occasions women were proud to show off their best clothes and jewelry. Often they paid professional photographers to take their pictures which would become treasured mementos to hang on their walls. I spent several hours recording events in and around the churchyard.

About midday the processions ended and I turned back toward my house, walking up the middle of the street because the narrow sidewalks were still choked with people. Just a few doors from my entrance a woman swept out from the crowd toward me. Smiling and wearing a black velvet *huipil* of a type usually worn during mourning and a long, filmy, rose floral skirt, she introduced herself.

"Francisca Maria del Refugio Lopez *para servirle*," she offered, extending her hand. "We are neighbors."

Suddenly a little shy and ill-at-ease as bystanders watched from the curb, she asked if I would accompany her to the fiesta in the afternoon. Momentarily surprised by her spontaneous invitation, I managed to recover my composure enough to introduce myself. She said she already knew who I was. We agreed to meet on the spot where we now stood in an hour. With this, Francisca Maria del Refugio Lopez sailed back into the crowd and disappeared. On the way back to my house, I reviewed this new experience, a woman seeking me out rather than the opposite. I did not recall seeing her before. Her costume was somewhat unusual, mourning huipil with fiesta skirt, but there was a flair for style about her that set her apart from her neighbors. She struck me as beautiful in a different way than most San Juan women; taller, and more slender, with more delicate features than was the local ideal of feminine beauty.

At the appointed hour I found her waiting, now wearing a proper burgundy velvet fiesta huipil and the same sheer rose skirt, bare toes peeking out from under the hemline. Her hair, still damp from bathing, was tightly braided and laced with rose satin ribbons in fiesta style. Even the taut, still-wet braids could not keep straying curls from asserting themselves at her neck and forehead. Many Zapotec people have beautiful black, wavy or curly hair which they consider wild and unattractive and try to "tame" with water and braids.

We walked down the street toward the house of the *mayordomo* (fiesta sponsor) at the far end of the pueblo. As we walked she took my arm as is the custom between Zapotec friends. She asked about my country, my family, my work, what I thought of her village. As with any good informant, she had the lively curiosity I found enchanting.

"My father lived in a place called Texas a long time ago, before I was born. Do you know where Texas is? Have you been there?" she asked.

Her father could speak English and had tried to teach her the language when she was a child but she was "too stupid" to learn, she lamented.

"Even Spanish I speak crooked, as I am sure you have noticed," she continued.

I liked her immediately, and complimented her on her Spanish which did not seem so "crooked" to me, remarking that it was certainly much better than mine. We talked and laughed about the language mistakes we both made and decided that similarity made us like sisters. By the time we reached the fiesta, I felt she was an acquaintance of long standing.

The street in front of the house hosting the fiesta was full of people. Men stood in knots, talking and laughing, around each of the three or four beer kiosks set up for the occasion. Women and girls hurried through the crowds of men in twos and threes. In San Juan women always pass through the streets swiftly, a way of discouraging gossip and possible unpleasant encounters with strange men and drunks. The obvious haste of the women gives outsiders the false impression that women are more industrious than men. Both sexes work long hours under difficult conditions, although there are also many opportunities for rest periods during the long days that often begin at 4:00 a.m. The fiestas are a major source of recreation for both men and women.

We forced our way through the crowds into the patio of the house, Francisca (hereafter called by her nickname, Chica) greeting friends and relatives on all sides. One of several village bands was playing "La Zandunga" as we entered. The music was loud, raucous, and dissonant, rendering the beautiful "Zandunga" almost painful to the ear.

My observations after attending public fiestas in El Centro and Xochitlan as well as a couple of weddings were indicating that "La Zandunga" had much deeper meaning in Zapotec culture than to put people into a festive mood. The piece was always played with great ceremony at particular junctures in the fiestas and the dance which sometimes accompanied it was a solemn, ceremonious rite. People did not laugh and joke when dancing "La Zandunga" and only certain people important to that particular fiesta danced it. At weddings "La Zandunga" was danced just once by the bride and groom, the *padrinos* and parents of the newlyweds, and perhaps a few specially revered relatives. The dance itself was entirely distinct from the social dancing that continued hour after hour at most fiestas. In "La Zandunga" couples did not touch but circled around one another, women holding their brightly embroidered skirts out prettily to show off the wide starched lace band (the *olan*) at the bottom. Men, usually dressed in the all-white costume of earlier times, wore a red kerchief around the neck and held their hands clasped behind their backs. No matter how many times "La Zandunga" was played during a fiesta, it was always repeated precisely at midnight. I was beginning to perceive that "La Zandunga" was something of a Zapotec national anthem. Although I was not a folklorist or musicologist, I placed "La Zandunga" on my mental list of subjects to investigate more thoroughly if time permitted.

When "La Zandunga" ended, the band struck up a lively Latin rhythm and the social dancing began. With several fiestas behind me, I was not surprised to see that most of the dancers were women. Characteristic of the region, women dance in couples while men watch from benches along one side, smoking cigarettes and drinking *mezcal*.

Chica asked me to dance and we circled the uneven dirt floor a few times. I apologized for my stumbling. Her bare feet slid over the ridges and depressions as though the surface were of glass. Observing the action and interactions was not possible while dancing and observation was what I was there for, so at the end of that number I asked to rest on the sidelines. Chica danced with several other women, including her sister. Because fiestas are a means of gaining and basking in one's social status, fiesta activities are dominated by gray-haired elders. Years of contributing their money and food to the fiestas of others and sponsoring fiestas themselves bring status and respect, while maturity gives one the time to enjoy it.

From time to time young girls, small children, and young men danced, almost always in same-gender pairs. I noted that the young men who were dancing were different from most of the young men I had seen on the streets. The dancing men were known as *muxe*, a legendary part of Isthmus Zapotec culture. Some wore rouge and lipstick, many wore gold necklaces and bracelets. Some had their hair dressed with more than masculine attention, with "spit curls" in front of the ears or across the forehead. One young man wore bright blue spike-heeled pumps. The muxe were dressed in items of feminine apparel but not that of Zapotec women, who never wore high heels, spit curls, or cosmetics.

The muxe danced with each other and with young women, usually their sisters and cousins. As I was to learn, muxes fill a third-gender place in the culture, between men and women, and in San Juan they are not scorned and ostracized as similar persons have been in our culture. Most spend their lives in the pueblo and family of their birth, integrated into the kinship system the same as other children.

At the very first fiesta I ever attended, I ran into a problem—no public bathrooms. I asked a nearby woman for the *baño*, and she proceeded to take me by the hand and lead me out into the street, where she indicated I should take care of my problem. This was going to be more of an ordeal than I anticipated with my knee-length tight skirt. Fortunately, on that occasion I was only a few blocks from my hotel and beat a hasty retreat to the shelter of my room. I was soon to observe that the street presented less of a problem to Zapotec women who could conceal themselves adequately with their long, full skirts, while relieving themselves. People walked past without taking the slightest notice. I changed to longer, fuller skirts, particularly for attending fiestas or taking trips which would require long hours away from home.

At the fiesta I was now attending with Chica, the need did not arise because we did not stay more than a couple of hours. We left the fiesta about 4:00 p.m., Chica explaining that she had to fix dinner for her mother, brother, and husband and shell corn to feed the pigs. As we walked home she told me she had been staying with her ill mother since her youngest sister married. Chica was the eldest daughter so it was her duty. She and her husband had closed their own small house near the market and now stayed with her mother. She longed to return to her own house but, without a daughter-in-law in her mother's house, she had no choice. In front of the church, Chica took her leave and disappeared through the doorway of a *cantina*.

About two weeks passed before I saw Chica again. Then one afternoon as I was typing field notes, she came to my house. We sat in the hammocks on the veranda, moving the hammocks to and fro with our feet as local custom dictates. I offered her a soft drink and for a few minutes we swung idly, sipping the sodas.

She asked if I liked the gold coin jewelry women wear at the fiestas. I replied that I found it very attractive but too expensive for me, guessing that she had some to sell. Women had frequently approached me in the street with offers to sell earrings or a necklace and I had collected some data on types and prices of the pieces for my research notes.

Chica reached into her skirt waistband and drew out a large kerchief containing some gold jewelry. Yes, she was selling them, she said, unfolding the cloth in her lap and handing me a gold pendant. They belonged to her mother and sister and had to be sold right away because her sister, Faustina, had required a caesarean section for the birth of her first child and the in-laws could not pay the large hospital bill. I admired the pieces but expressed my regret that there was no fund in my research account for gold jewelry. Obviously disappointed, she tucked the wad carefully back into her waistband, adjusted her huipil to cover it and slipped out the gate and down the hill as silently and gracefully as an eagle gliding on the edge of a downwind.

The days ran imperceptibly into each other. Soon after the patron saint's fiesta, Lent began. Now there were no more Sunday weddings with their fireworks and music to act as my weekly time-markers. Church weddings and other fiestas are taboo all through Lent.

My entrance gate was at the foot of the hill about 150 yards away and therefore it was difficult to hear people knocking. One midday while typing field notes, I gradually became aware of a furious pounding on the gate below. Hurrying down the hill cursing the mischievous little boys who had twice torn out the electric buzzer, I pulled away the heavy pole which kept the latchless gate closed. With effort I pushed the eight-foot-high gate open just enough for a person to squeeze through. Nobody entered. I opened wider. Chica, smiling broadly, stood there holding a baby in her arms.

"Here is my daughter Terecita. You are going to be her godmother, *verdad*?"

The infant was her month-old niece, daughter of Faustina, the baby born by the caesarean surgery which had required the sale of the jewelry.

"Maybe," I hedged. "When?" I asked as she stepped into the yard.

"*Vamonos* next Thursday to the Cathedral in El Centro."

I explained that I was not a Catholic. What would the priest say?

"Never mind that. He won't ask."

After some discussion I agreed to become Terecita's *madrina* for this, her first communion. She already had a madrina of baptism (the most important madrina), acquired when she was but a few days old. The baby was large and plump, with enormous jet black eyes and a mass of black ringlets. Already she was a charmer.

On Thursday, as planned, we went in the pick-up truck to get the baby. I met Faustina, mother of Terecita, for the first time. After the church ceremony she and I would be *comadres* (co-parents). I had brought the new clothing which custom requires of the madrina. We sat in the hammocks and waited while Faustina dressed her daughter in these, exclaiming all the while:

"Ay, what precious shoes! How beautiful this dress! What fine taste has my comadre!"

The two sisters did not resemble one another. Chica was tall and quite slim, with delicate features and curly hair. Faustina, fifteen years her junior, was short and plump, with a light complexion, straight brown-black hair, and a round, full face.

Taking the newly attired baby, Chica and I left for the cathedral. Once there we found the place completely deserted. We waited for a while in the corredor before a woman came out to tell us that Thursday baptisms and communions had been discontinued. We would have to return on Sunday. I tried to conceal my annoyance that most of the day had been wasted, blaming myself for not confirming the date independently. By now I should have realized that I was probably the only person in the entire region who was concerned with time.

The following Sunday we managed to get the baby to the cathedral, although late because of a dead battery in the pick-up. The place was alive with people, most carrying babies and small children. Chica and I took turns holding Terecita who slept soundly through the noise and commotion. After a few minutes of shifting Terecita from arm to arm, apparently trying to wake her, Chica said sadly, "This baby is going to die." The infant continued to sleep.

"Why do you say that?" I asked, puzzled. Terecita seemed healthy enough to me.

"Look!" She held the baby up and shook her gently. Terecita opened her eyes and gazed sleepily at her aunt.

"Look at her! She doesn't cry!"

I suggested the baby was just sleepy.

"No, that's not it. I can tell if they are going to die. I can always tell." Chica stared off across the courtyard filled with crying babies, preoccupied with her own thoughts. Terecita was already sleeping again.

We waited on into the stifling afternoon. At last we were ushered into the cathedral and placed in one of two lines, that of madrinas with baby girls. Padrinos with baby boys made up the other line. The priest was moving down the boys' line baptizing and giving communion far up toward the front of the church. We were at the rear, near the end of the girls' line. By now Terecita had begun screaming with great energy. Nothing I did quieted her. I glanced over my shoulder at Chica sitting several rows behind us. She was beaming. The priest moved fast, urged on by dozens of crying infants. Soon he was before us, reading the name of the baby from the list he held, sprinkling holy water and moving on to the next. Chica sailed forward, swept the still screaming Terecita from my arms and turned toward the doorway, triumphant.

On the way back to Faustina's house across the river, Terecita fell into an exhausted sleep while we talked.

"Why did you say this baby, my *ahijada*, is going to die?" I asked.

Chica's face darkened. "Who should know better than I about babies dying? So many times I have seen my children die! They always look fat and healthy but they do not cry. And then they die, in a few hours or a few days but they always die."

I had heard that several of Chica's infants had died soon after birth. I asked how many children she had lost.

"How many?" She hesitated, counting them by name on her fingers. "Eight, no, nine I think. Now it is hard to remember. I will ask Anastasio when he comes home. He remembers."

As we drove, Chica continued talking. Anastasio was her eldest child, age seventeen, one of two living children. Both sons were attending a Protestant mission school in Veracruz. Anastasio had been there for three years, his thirteen-year-old brother Alberto for less than a year. Most of her relatives and neighbors thought it was scandalous that she had allowed them to become Protestants. But the gringo evangelists came one day to San Juan and asked boys in the streets if they wanted to get an education, live in a nice house, and eat good food everyday. Anastasio was fourteen, and he wanted to go. His uncle, Chica's brother who had been educated in Mexico City, thought it was a good idea too. Only Anastasio and one other San Juan boy of the same age went. The school was just being established. People said it was a ruse, that the boys would be treated badly, become slaves to the gringos and not get any education at all. Chica and her husband Catarino had thought long and deeply about it before making a decision. Even after three years she still had misgivings sometimes.

She missed her sons so much it was almost unbearable at times. But what chance had they here in San Juan, running wild in the streets, skipping school, not learning a trade? Here they would come to no good end, probably end up borrachos. If they had stayed in San Juan, they would be forever poor and miserable like she was, Chica concluded.

Chica admired the gringos at the mission school because they did not allow the boys to roam the streets, they saw that they attended school regularly and they taught them to study the Bible, taught them to make things with their hands and to raise some of their own food. The boys were forbidden to drink, smoke, or swear, and they were taught to be courteous to everyone. Now her neighbors were jealous when the boys returned during school vacations neatly dressed and polite, their progress in school obvious.

Chica herself no longer believed in the saints, she confided, because now her sons were Protestants and she wanted to be one too. Protestants did not believe in the saints. What did I think about that, she asked, giving me a sidelong glance. She used to believe in the saints, burning candles and praying all the time, and still her children died—at birth, at two months, one even at two years, but they all died. The saints were no help at all. She fell silent as we neared the house of my new comadre and her in-laws.

5

Miracles and Mangoes

A saintmaker lived in San Juan. Down the street a few doors from Tiu Tono's, an old Guatemalan rented a cubbyhole of a room in the front of the baker's house, where he lived and created his saints. For months I admired his beautiful saints, hand-carved of wood and carefully painted, their glass eyes and genuine hair eyelashes making them so eerily lifelike. Every few days he displayed a different saint in his doorway. They were true works of art and I vowed that before I left San Juan one would be mine. Since my personal non-grant funds were limited, I thought it prudent to put off buying the saint until near the end of my stay. I mentioned my plan to Chica.

"Oh, don't pay all that money! I will give you my saint," was her response.

I promptly forgot her offer, but a few days later she came to my house, clutching a tall object swathed in a white cloth.

"Here is your saint, Sacred Heart of Jesus," she smiled, unveiling with a flourish the plaster-of-paris figurine about two feet tall. I appreciated her generous gesture even though I still intended to buy the hand-carved saint before I left. Sacred Heart thereafter reigned over my household altar where before there was only a picture of a saint. Chica admired him in his new home.

"Oh, I do not need a saint, because I am no longer Catholic," she assured me. "He has been packed away in my trunk for a long time."

Only a few days later as the two of us passed a little chapel at the far end of the pueblo she pulled me toward the entrance.

"Let's pray to San Marcial so people won't think we are Protestants!"

San Marcial helped people find lost articles, his specialty being

Brothers, 1982

lost animals. We entered the dark little dirt-floored chapel, lit a candle, and dropped a coin in the box provided for offerings.

"What have you lost? What shall I pray for?" Chica wanted to know.

I had not realized we were going to pray for *my* lost articles so I thought fast and requested a prayer for some papers I had misplaced. I located the papers a few days later. Zapotec friends thought it was another sign confirming San Marcial's powers while I privately interpreted it as coincidence.

Chica's ambivalence in religious matters was not unique in San Juan. Most people were nominally Catholic, publicly mildly anti-Protestant, yet few were either fervently Catholic or fanatically unilateral in religious practices and beliefs. Tiu Tono no longer believed in the saints and did not hesitate to say so publicly. Roberto, the potter, and the other potter families, recent converts to Jehovah's Witnesses, no longer participated in the fiesta system, yet people accepted them and refrained from criticizing their new religion except for their tiresome habit of going door-to-door selling the *Watchtower* and "talking evangelism." Most people utilized whatever means available when it came to dealing with supernatural forces. The saints and fiestas remained important in most people's lives but officials of the Catholic Church, like the official Church itself, were generally mistrusted. San Juan seldom had a resident priest, hiring priests from El Centro as needed to conduct wedding and funeral masses. Otherwise people took care of their own religious needs with Zapotec lay religious specialists. The saints were what counted for most people and anyone could pray and make offerings and promises to the saints.

The saints were especially important in crisis situations. When a family member was ill and other treatments did not bring the expected results, the family made a vow to honor a particular saint with a fiesta, a pilgrimage, or in extreme cases, a chapel constructed in his honor if the saint would but cure the loved one. All of the three chapels in San Juan had been built as fulfillments of promises and many sponsors of fiestas to patron saints were fulfilling past promises to a saint by acting as mayordomos and paying the heavy expenses that office involved.

When asked to sponsor a child at a Catholic ceremony, I always carefully explained to the parents that I was not Catholic. If the ceremony required that I sign a statement to the effect that I was

Catholic, I informed them that I would not be able to sponsor the child. Such statements are required for baptisms and marriages but not for communions. My several compadre relationships were therefore all created through sponsorship of a child's communion.

Although I worried about it before beginning fieldwork, my being non-Catholic did not seem to bother anyone in San Juan. They never inquired about my religion although I also explained that I was not an evangelista (Fundamental Protestant). Some people did not trust the evangelistas who came from time to time to talk against the cherished folk religious practices of the residents of San Juan and to try to convert people to their "better" way. Ethnocentricity and lack of insight into and appreciation of the culture of those they hoped to convert, were major failings of the evangelistas in my judgment.

As I was returning home at dusk one evening not long after our visit to the shrine of San Marcial, a shadowy figure moved toward me through the dark passageway to the pueblo.

"*Ma zeedu la*?" came a familiar voice, using the Zapotec greeting equivalent to our how-do-you-do.

Surprised to see Chica headed toward El Centro so late, I asked if someone was sick.

"*Ay, Dios*! I have to go see about my mangoes. There are no trucks to take them to Oaxaca. Three days now I hunt for a driver and there are none, because everyone has mangoes to transport."

She was distraught. The mangoes, twelve baskets of them, had been sitting in the sun on the sidewalk in front of the market for three days. She told me she had been making two trips a day to El Centro to check on them and thought they would only endure one more day. If she did not find a trucker to haul them tomorrow they would be pig feed! She seemed ready to cry. I put my arm around her shoulder and asked if I could help.

"Maybe we can take them in the pick-up," I heard myself offering.

"Is it possible? Will the *camioneta* hold them?" She brightened.

Ignorance is bliss, as the saying goes. At that moment I was still woefully ignorant of the size of mango baskets (comparable to a thirty-gallon garbage can) and I never imagined that mangoes were so heavy! For the time being I remained joyfully unaware of all the implications of my ill-considered and hasty offer. I told her we would try it. At least we could take part of them.

"*Bueno*," Chica agreed. She would come to my house ready to leave at daybreak. Now she had to hurry home to wash and iron her clothes for the trip. I suspected the clothes she would wash were the ones she was wearing. In the weeks since we met I had become aware that Chica had fewer clothes than the other San Juan women I knew. She seemed to have only three skirts and tops, and only one of these was in good enough condition to wear to public events. From this observation I guessed that she was in fairly dire financial straits. San Juan women love pretty clothes and take pride in dressing well. In spite of her small wardrobe, Chica herself was fastidious in personal grooming and always wore freshly laundered garments.

The next morning Chica arrived with her husband, Cata, whom I had not yet met. Would I mind if he went with us? That way, he could load and unload the mangoes instead of paying a porter.

Cata was much darker in complexion than Chica and a couple of inches shorter, with straight bristly black hair. He was shy and self-conscious. Since he spoke only Zapotec, Chica had to act as our mutual translator.

Each mango-filled basket must have weighed close to two hundred pounds and, on seeing them, I doubted that my little six-cylinder pick-up truck could carry the load one hundred and fifty-six uphill miles to Oaxaca. Cata, lean but strong, loaded all twelve baskets without help. It was touch-and-go to get them all into the small bed of the pick-up. Noting that the truck's springs were sagging ominously, I crossed my fingers and tried to conceal my dismay at the overload. If ever I needed the help of the saints it was now, I thought, trying my best to appear cheerful and confident before my two guests.

Thus began the long, sinuous ascent to the mile-high city of Oaxaca. At every depression in the road I winced as truck springs met axle with a disturbing clank. I anticipated the worst—a broken axle, flat tires—if something broke, we could go careening down a canyon, the frequent fate of public buses. Not one normally given to praying, I silently did so now.

As we crawled up the highway in second gear, Cata and Chica chatted excitedly in Zapotec. From time to time Chica would translate something into Spanish for my benefit. Cata had never been to Oaxaca although as a young man he had served two years in the military in Mexico City and Veracruz. Chica had been to Oaxaca to sell mangoes for the past few years, making several trips each season. I commented that she probably knew more about Oaxaca than I did. No, she said, she did not know anything at all about the city except the street where mangoes were sold. She just got off the bus and walked to that street and when the fruit was sold she walked the few blocks back to the bus terminal and waited for the next bus home.

I suggested that we take a little holiday after selling the mangoes to celebrate our good luck in getting them to Oaxaca (providing we did get them there). We could go to the archaeological sites of Monte Alban and Mitla and visit the famous colonial cathedral. They were enthusiastic. Chica had heard about the cathedral from relatives and said she always wanted to see it for herself.

We arrived in Oaxaca at noon, already late for the day's best selling hours. Cata unloaded the twelve baskets of fruit while a uniformed policeman told me I was in trouble because I lacked a license to haul mangoes. I suppose he was trying for a *mordida* (bribe) but I played the dumb gringa who had difficulty understanding him and he eventually walked away. There were several other women from San Juan selling mangoes nearby. Cata was the only man around except for the policeman and an occasional porter. I went to check into a hotel a few blocks away to rest, exhausted from the mental and physical strain of the long drive. Promising to check on them in a couple of hours, I suggested that if they sold the mangoes before I returned they could come over to the hotel. Neither Chica nor Cata could read the street signs so they both felt insecure and timid in the city. What if they got lost? I drew them a map to the hotel and wrote the name and address.

"Just show this paper to a person on the street," I suggested. Chica was sure nobody would be able to understand her Spanish.

"They will understand you," I reassured, "but just show them the paper."

When I returned they were in the same spot, still surrounded by most of their mangoes. I could see it was going to take at least another day to sell them. Usually mangoes from the south sell briskly and bring a good price at this season because local mangoes are not yet ripe. A woman can normally anticipate netting about double what she would get by selling the fruit at home, so most women opt for the long, tiring bus trips to Oaxaca once or twice a week during mango season.

A woman called to Chica from several spaces down. I asked who she was. Chica showed extraordinary patience with my tiresome questions. She already knew that "Who is that?" actually meant to whom is she related, where does she live, is she your relative or comadre, and what does she do to earn money? She began telling me the woman's background. Chica could be an effusive talker although she was anything but compulsive about it. Sometimes she was quiet and sad, lost in her own problems. Today she was in one of her happier moods, pleased to be selling her mangoes. It occurred to me that she might be able to help with some questionnaires because she was so quick to fathom the kinds of information I wanted and she intuitively seemed to understand what I was trying to accomplish with the research in spite of what were probably my inadequate explanations.

After a couple of hours I went back to the hotel with the understanding that they would be my guests for dinner. Chica said they could not go to a restaurant because they had no place to bathe and change clothes so I offered my room.

That evening when we arrived at the restaurant, Cata and Chica were nervous. Neither of them had eaten in a restaurant where customers were expected to use forks and knives.

"Just eat like you do at home," I suggested. "Nobody will notice and anyway we are here to enjoy ourselves. Why should we care about what strangers think?"

We ordered food and a bottle of beer around. Chica insisted on using her fork. The cecina was tough and served in one large piece. They struggled to cut it with a fork and knife. We all laughed and I demonstrated how to hold the utensils to make it easy. I finished and they said they could eat no more, though their plates were still full of food. They looked uncomfortable and embarrassed. Chica leaned over and whispered that she wanted to take the uneaten food with her. Mexican restaurants do not furnish "doggy bags" so I helped her wrap the dry items in the end of her rebozo. The moist items I dropped in a plastic bag I always carried in my purse for just such occasions. Cata was fidgeting and looking at his feet.

They spent the night in the canopied bed of my pick-up parked in front of the hotel. Luckily, the police did not discover what was probably an infraction of city regulations.

Only the next day did I learn that their lack of appetite in the restaurant was a result of their having eaten at the market beforehand because they were afraid they would not like the exotic restaurant food. Cata had been mortified at our taking the leftover food with us and had scolded Chica about it later. He said we reminded him of turkey vultures clamoring over an animal carcass. I stoutly defended our actions, telling them that was the regular custom in my country and I did not care what complete strangers thought about us.

"Yes," said Chica, "you can fly in the face of others' opinions because you are a rich gringa. But humildes (poor people) like us have to be careful of our actions and the impression we make on others." I understood that she meant mestizos could embarrass them with unkind put-downs if they were to draw attention to themselves here in this unfamiliar city environment.

Usually men do not accompany their wives to the Oaxaca market or any other. Market-selling is women's business. Chica later told me she had persuaded Cata to come to help load and unload because they had a free ride and because when he was left alone he was apt to go on a drinking spree.

The trip to Oaxaca marked the beginning of a closer relationship between Chica and me. A few days later, I went with her to the orchards to spend the day cutting mangoes. We left by oxcart before sunrise—Chica, a hired twenty-year-old neighbor, a twelve-year-old nephew, and two nieces age nineteen and thirteen. Cata had gone on earlier to his own fields where he and his brother would cut their mangoes. Toward sundown Cata and his brother would come by with their cartloads of mangoes and we would all return home together.

On our way out of the pueblo, we stopped to allow the nineteen-year-old 'Stiana to deliver some food her mother had sent to a comadre. As we waited, a young man leaning against a wall said something to Pedro, the hired hand, and before we knew what was happening the two of them were locked in a wrestling match in the street. Chica grabbed the reins to the oxen and tried to keep them calm, meanwhile shouting to the returning 'Stiana to hurry up and separate these two "*pendejos*." 'Stiana ran into the fray and forcibly pulled the two men apart, then wedged herself between the two and held them apart, all the while scolding them as only Zapotec women can scold. I was surprised that 'Stiana, a nineteen-year-old unmarried girl, would have the temerity and strength to act as referee in a conflict between men. I was even more surprised that the two young men accepted her referee position without protest. Pedro dusted himself off, got back on the cart and we continued our journey as if nothing unusual had happened. What the fight was about I never learned. Pedro seemed more interested in knowing if he appeared to be winning before the two were separated. The youngsters had fun teasing me: "Hey, Bevi, why didn't you separate them?" they laughed. I tried to imagine the same situation at home. A woman trying to separate two fighting men could expect to be knocked out of the way in short order and told it was none of her business. Here the men seemed to cooperate in not resisting the effort to separate them.

This incident was another in a growing number of clues that women's informal roles in peace-keeping and conflict resolution were an important part of Zapotec culture. After this incident, I began to pay closer attention to women's spontaneous and seemingly casual roles as conflict resolvers and peacekeepers.

* * *

Shortly after I moved into Tiu Tono's house relations between me and Tiu Tono began to cool. Only a few days after my move he informed me that I was not acting like a proper daughter of the house when I sat on his stoop in the evenings chatting with neighbors. In following weeks he let me know that he thought I was having too many visitors and their banging on the gate bothered him. I thought I was not having nearly enough "visitors," people who came for the informal chats which had replaced my first attempts at more formal scheduled home interviews.

The good news was that I was making real progress in getting to know many people in San Juan. To avoid annoying my landlord, in late afternoons I sometimes joined the women and children who sat on the stoop in front of Soledad's cantina, just out of sight of the disapproving Tiu Tono. Chica was not often present because she had evening chores, but sometimes her mother Lucia felt strong enough to venture out. Soledad, the *cantinera*, was introduced to me as Lucia's niece, although later while collecting family genealogies I discovered that she was really Lucia's late husband's second cousin. Etiquette in San Juan requires that everyone of any relationship be addressed by the closest kin term appropriate for their age and sex.

Soledad was thirty-two years old, four years Chica's junior, big, bluff, and perpetually scowling. She was raised an only child, considered by everyone to be a great handicap. She had run the cantina ever since she was orphaned at age eighteen. Sole ran a tight cantina and she was proud of it, brooking no nonsense from clients, sober or borracho, though she was always a little on the defensive about her livelihood. Maybe it was not a proper living for a woman, she said, but she had to look after herself and her five children. Could she be choosy? The cantina provided a comfortable living.

Soledad's children's father, twenty years her senior, spent most of his time on the premises, though he was not her legal husband and had a legitimate family just down the street. Theirs was, in anthropological terms, half of a polygynous family; not unheard of in San Juan but unusual in that the two families lived in close proximity. She and Don Sebio seemed to get along well most of the time. She lost her patience only when he took money from the cantina and gave it to his legal family. That was what sent her into a rage, Soledad said.

Lucia told me that the last time this had happened, Soledad had become wild with anger, throwing Don Sebio's belongings into the street and shouting obscenities. Don Sebio, a large, strongly built man, meekly accepted the verbal barrage, gathered his things, and left. It was apparently weeks, perhaps months, before Sole would consider accepting his apologies. Poor man, sighed Doña Lucia, he had made the rounds of all of Sole's relatives and comadres, soliciting palancas to persuade Sole to forgive him. What touched her, said Doña Lucia, were the big tears that would well up in his eyes and overrun his leathery cheeks as he pleaded his case with various relatives. Was it not a sad thing to see a strong man weep? Lucia shook her head in sympathy.

Sole's stern scowl was mostly a front. Her heart was as soft as tortilla dough and she had eventually accepted Don Sebio back again. Now, she said, she was just tired of this cantina business, forever selling beer to borrachos. She especially disliked selling beer in the streets at the fiestas, her major moneymaker. What she really wanted to do was to make trips to Mexico City to buy manufactured clothing and resell it in small, remote villages in the hills. That was the good life, to be always going here and there, buying and selling. She would have done it long ago but for the children being so small and the fact that she could not read or write. She thought she would have to be literate to be a viajera. Don Sebio had tried to teach her, God knows, but when one is grown up it is too late to learn things, she sighed.

Doña Lucia complained that her son did not like to see the women of his family sitting idly in the street, but was she not entitled to get out in the cool air once in a while? After all, she would soon be dead and cold in the cemetery, so why not enjoy life a little yet?

Gradually, through these informal talk sessions I was learning a great deal about the people and culture of San Juan, learning who was related to whom, what worries these women had, what made them happy or sad, and I was picking up more of the Zapotec language. For the first time in all the months I had been here, I began to feel that in a small way I belonged.

Ten to fifteen more household questionnaires were needed. Who would help me? Chica would be an excellent interpreter and assistant but she had so many cares that I hesitated to ask. Still, she was quick to grasp my explanations of what information I wanted and she was well-liked in the community. Besides she was an excellent translator-interpreter of Zapotec, something of an art that not all people can master, I had found. I finally found the courage to ask her. I would pay her, of course, just as I had Betina. She responded that she would be happy to help me but could not accept pay from a friend. I preferred a formal arrangement of paying for her time because she obviously needed money and I thought we would get more done by treating the work as a regular job.

I kept a faithful account of her hours during the weeks she was helping me but she steadfastly refused to accept money. An informal arrangement developed whereby she "borrowed" a hundred pesos or so when she needed them. The rest I put aside, planning to give it to her in a lump sum when I left the field.

Usually she could get away only long enough to complete one questionnaire and that not daily. She would plan ahead who we should see next and put out feelers beforehand as to whether they would be cooperative. She helped me complete the house-count census, making it more accurate because she knew when several households shared a single entrance.

I had an extra gate key made for her so that she could enter my house whenever she wished without banging on the gate that so annoyed Tiu Tono. She kept the key tied to the waistband of her skirt and, although she seldom used it, I knew she was immensely pleased that I trusted her to such a degree. The key seemed to be an important symbol of our friendship which she could display to relatives and friends.

One midday as she and I were returning from an interview, we heard the staccato rap of firecrackers nearby. I paid no attention as fireworks are set off almost daily as announcements for various private and public fiestas. Chica, though, was more alert and quickly jerked me into a recessed doorway. What I thought were firecrackers were shots fired from a real pistol held by a very real, very drunk man standing in the doorway of a cantina a few doors up the street. As I so suddenly learned that day, an unaware passerby has a good chance of being killed in San Juan by such drunken displays of machismo. We waited cautiously in the doorway. Soon the municipio presidente edged his way along the wall up the street toward the cantina, and persuaded the man to surrender his firearm. We continued on our way. After that I was alert to drunken men and the sound of "firecrackers" when I passed through the streets alone.

Slowly we would complete the questionnaires and the house census, sandwiching these tasks between going to Oaxaca to sell mangoes (though never again in the pick-up), to Xochitlan to sell bananas, Doña Lucia's "bad" days when Chica could not leave the house, funerals and fiestas. Concurrently I carried on the other activities I could do on my own.

One of these was talking to Doña Lucia on her good days. She, like her daughter, was an astute observer of her own culture who could tell me many things about "the old days," about her life, and about the pueblo and its people. Chica was a top-rate informant in her own right, and we spent hours talking while she worked or we rested in the hammocks during siestas.

Chica came to depend on me for advice and confided some of her deepest thoughts and anxieties. One day she remarked that she thought she had diabetes like her mother because she was always thirsty. I offered to accompany her to a doctor but she refused, saying it was better not to go because she could never afford all the medication, the daily injections, and the blood transfusions her mother frequently required.

Chica felt very badly about not having more living children. The doctor had told her during her last parturition two years earlier that to become pregnant again would be to risk her life. He had given her a sample of birth control pills but she quit taking them when the sample was gone because they were so expensive at the pharmacy. She felt useless because she was unable to bear more children, she opined. (She had produced ten children in less than twenty years of marriage though only two had lived). As a woman, she confided, she was a failure, good for nothing! I reminded her that she had two healthy, well-behaved boys, nearly grown, which she should be very proud of, but she was not consoled. The eight who were dead weighed on her mind. Remembering, she would become despondent. I tried to avoid this painful subject but she returned to it again and again, preoccupied with what she saw as one of life's most bitter defeats.

6

Fiestas and Fieldwork

The fiestas are the most cherished customs of Isthmus Zapotecs and the first events a visitor will be invited to witness. There are community fiestas for the patron saints of the churches and there are private rites-of-passage fiestas—weddings, funerals, and the many death memorial rites. Even though all these are referred to as "fiestas" they do not all have the festive air we usually associate with the word. What they all have in common is their religious significance. Although they may not appear so to outsiders, all are sacred events. Fiestas serve the subsidiary but important function of recreation and relief from the monotonous routine of daily living. Community fiestas and weddings are joyous occasions with dancing, drinking, and eating as all integral parts of the rituals. Funerals and commemorative death rituals (*mixa gue'tu'*) include eating and drinking but are less joyous occasions and do not include dancing and general merrymaking.

While one does not need an invitation to most public fiestas, I was invited to one near my hotel during my first week in the field. Not long afterward Leonzo arranged for me to go to a wedding in San Juan. Jonsa, his wife, was not attending and it would have been improper for Leonzo and me to go together, so he arranged for me to go with his "sister." She dutifully allowed me to tag along but since she did not speak Spanish and I did not speak Zapotec there was not much I could learn at this wedding except by observation. When, two days later, Leonzo remarked that he was an only child, I asked who the lady was with whom I went to the fiesta. She was his first cousin, he explained, and one's cousins are always respected by calling them sisters and brothers. Just a few days later Leonzo and Jonsa took me with them to a funeral in a neighboring town. There were many later opportunities to attend all types of fiestas.

Taking mental notes and photographs if the hosts allowed it and asking dozens of questions, I gradually learned the pattern of seating and the timing and sequence of the series of little ceremonies within each fiesta. Weddings have their particular sequence of small rituals within the larger fiesta, as do funerals and fiestas to patron saints. Next I learned what various participants were expected to do, when, and why, and what each class of participant was expected to contribute in money and other items.

One of the first things I noted about the fiestas was that men and women were always segregated. The men sat on long benches along one side of the enclosure. Close by the entrance was the "saint's table" over which the mayordomo and other fiesta principals presided. Here each man paid his contribution as he entered, receiving a shot of mezcal and a cigarette in return. His name and contribution were duly entered in a ledger and then all of the men toasted the contributor and the patron saint by drinking a shot of mezcal. In the course of a few hours men imbibe enormous quantities of mezcal and smoke several cigarettes, although few smoke at any other time. As the day wears on most of the men become stone drunk. This is one of the least desirable aspects of the fiestas, in my view, because it starts many men on the road to alcoholism, perhaps the major social problem in the area.

Women also pay a contribution, although less than the men, and receive grape juice as a toast. Women do not drink mezcal nor are they required to toast each woman as she pays. Beer is the drink of choice for women at fiestas and, like the men's mezcal and cigarettes, is paid for by the sponsors of the fiesta. A woman can drink a rather large quantity of beer during a fiesta if so inclined, because the host and hostess never allow anyone to be without a bottle in hand. However, ordinarily women get no more than mildly tipsy and rarely become alcoholic. Drinking beer outside the context of the fiestas is considered unbecoming, even scandalous, behavior for women.

Not surprisingly, as the fiesta day wears on a few men usually begin to act in inappropriate ways. They may try to dance with the women when only women are supposed to be dancing or shout obscenities and start fights. After observing a number of fiestas I noted that the order-keepers within the fiesta were always matronly women, but when I asked people who policed the fiestas they always gave the same answer: male guards were posted at the entrances to take care of disturbances. How was I to reconcile this with my observations? The discrepancy seemed to lie in the difference between ideal behavior as dictated by the culture and real behavior as observed by the ethnographer. There were male guards but they were only functional at the entrances and beyond. Women's roles as peacekeepers within the fiesta were informal and hence not part of people's perception. I duly noted this in my field diary. As research continued I learned much more about this aspect of the culture.

The whole fiesta system is underwritten by an elaborate system of reciprocal obligations. People contribute to as many fiestas as possible whether or not they attend because these contributions act as credits that the contributors can draw on when they must give a fiesta. This is especially true of rite-of-passage fiestas (funerals and weddings) which every family will be obliged to give sooner or later. Contributors to fiestas gain community prestige by their contributions, but the highest levels of status and prestige accrue to those households who sponsor public patron saint fiestas. Families may go deeply in debt in order to sponsor a public fiesta and gain the community's respect and deference in return. Of course, only a relatively few families can sponsor such expensive events but most hope to give respectably bountiful death and wedding fiestas and thus gain some standing in the community, if not the very highest standing.

As a reflection of the size and expense of the fiestas, the few items below were selected from a long list of expenditures and contributions for a single wedding:

Expenses of Hosts:

Orchestras—three, for five days' playing
Beef—two live animals
Beer—350 cases
Mezcal—one hundred liters
Pork—three live animals
Firewood—four cartloads

Received from contributors:

Eggs—approximately one hundred dozen
Live chickens—seventy-eight
Cacao beans—approximately five kilos
Sugar—approximately thirty kilos

Zapotec wedding fiestas are not so much a celebration by the newlyweds as a celebration by the families of which the newlyweds are the central figures. In the old days when parents chose their children's mates, there existed the humiliating ritual of deflowering the virgin bride. Today the couple usually elopes to avoid this, then each returns to their home to plan a wedding which takes place a few weeks later. Even in their more abbreviated modern form, weddings are more for the elders than for the marrying couple. The newlyweds spend the entire day after the church mass going through ritual after ritual surrounded by their elder relatives, padrinos, and neighbors. Contemporaries of the bride and groom have but a peripheral part in the affair; the young women serving food, the young men setting off fireworks in the street at the appropriate times. One of the internal rituals of weddings is the *mediu xiga*, a ceremony in which the couple is seated in the center of the patio with a half-gourd container on their laps (mediu xiga means half gourd). Guests dance around them to a special tune bearing the title of the ritual, tossing money in the half-gourd and pasting bills on the newlyweds' foreheads or tucking coins into their hair and clothing. At the conclusion of mediu xiga the padrino counts the money received and announces the couple's "take" to all the guests over the loudspeaker, to bursts of enthusiastic applause.

The major art forms of Isthmus Zapotecs are not handicrafts but music and literature. The fiestas provide a public sounding board for newly composed songs and poetry. Musicians, especially those who compose their own songs, are greatly admired. Except for certain small rituals performed in preparation for the fiestas where Zapotec tunes are played to the accompaniment of flute and drum, modern fiesta music is entirely post-Contact and of European origin as are the modern musical instruments. Several literate Zapotec historians have researched some of the regional songs, especially the two best-loved, "La Llorona" (Weeping Woman) and "La Zandunga." According to their research, both of these melodies were introduced from the national capital in the 19th century. The most mysterious of the two is "La Zandunga," apparently first popularized in mid-century by a well-loved Zapotec clarinetist and bandleader, Máximo Ramon Ortiz, whose name appears in one of the many stanzas.

There are several versions and many stanzas of "La Zandunga," and there are differing opinions about the significance and meanings of the allegorical verses. Nobody is even certain who "La Zandunga" is or was. Was she a sweetheart, someone's mother, or the Zapotec symbol of all femininity? Perhaps "La Zandunga" represents the Zapotec ethos, the very spirit of Zapotec culture? Whatever her original form and meaning, there is no doubt that today "La Zandunga" represents Zapotec culture, all that which makes Zapotecs, as a people, unique. "La Zandunga" has become the Zapotec anthem. Hearing it, particularly in ceremonial contexts, can bring a lump to the throat and a tear to the eye.

All fiestas, both private and public, are considered to be community services because they honor the saints and ancestors, who will in turn look with favor on the future of the pueblo and its inhabitants. Very poor families are unable to gather sufficient resources to gain status through the system. Economically successful families, through Herculean efforts and expenditures, can climb the ladder to social success by the fiesta route.

As a participant in fiestas I must have been pretty much of a disappointment to people from the start. First of all, I was not much of a dancer, and for ethnographic reasons I preferred to sit on the sidelines and observe. Then, while all the women were drinking one bottle of beer after another, I nursed a single bottle all day long. The communal meals, usually two per fiesta, were something of a trial. All the women (and men in their turn) file into a room in which a long table is set up. There are no chairs. Bowls of hot beef in mole are served with a mountain of tortillas as the only utensils. While standing, one is supposed to be able to dip pieces of tortilla into the hot mole and bring it to the mouth without dripping or getting any mole on the fingers. Mole is colored red with achiote, the same plant material the South American Indians use to paint their bodies—it is not only bright red but also quite an effective permanent dye. I always ended the meal with achiote stains on my clothing and, worse, under my fingernails, marking me as an inept eater. People could tell when

I last attended a fiesta just by looking at my fingernails. My incompetence at dancing, beer-drinking, and dipping mole did not enhance my reputation as a party girl—something I perceived my hosts thought of as the minimal requirement for a foreign guest.

Rather quickly I learned that fiestas can consume vast quantities of the ethnographer's time. A modest wedding begins at 8:00 a.m. Sunday and lasts well into the night. An elaborate wedding can continue for three days and nights. Events for a patron saint begin a month before the saint's day, with some important event taking place at least once a week. During the week of the saint's day, there are usually at least three full days of rituals and festive activities. Funerals for strangers required me to spend most of a day away from other research, but for family members of informants considerably more participation and time was necessary.

In response to the pressures of getting data more important for my project, I soon found I had to decline fiesta invitations unless they were of special importance to one of my friends or comadres. Sometimes it was difficult to explain my decision to people. They love their fiestas and take great pride in the beauty of the costumes and the pageantry of the processions and rituals. Declining an invitation can be considered a rejection of them as individuals and families and their culture as well. The anthropologist, although sometimes viewed as naive and bungling, is inevitably regarded as a person of high status—a visiting dignitary. Because of this, declining invitations to fiestas requires some diplomacy. Explaining the constraints of time and money necessary to complete my research usually sufficed but inevitably a few people interpreted my non-attendance as a personal rejection.

Anthropological fieldwork should always be a two-way process. I was there to learn about their culture and collect information. The people who helped me rightfully expected to receive something in return. They did not often expect money or gifts, but rather intangibles such as the prestige of having the anthropologist present at their fiestas as an honored guest, or the status some felt they acquired by being seen in her presence, or by gaining her consent to sponsor a child in a Catholic ritual. After I was familiar with the fiestas, I found that appearing briefly at a wedding or death fiesta was sometimes sufficient to demonstrate my respect and goodwill and to repay people in a small way for tolerating me.

Of all the rituals I witnessed, those dealing with death proved the most exotic and interesting. When a family member dies, Zapotecs do not just have a funeral and end it at that. The funeral only marks the beginning of a series of commemorative fiestas for the deceased. These fiestas occur on the forty-day anniversary of death, at the one-year anniversary, and at several later anniversaries. The funeral rites and commemorative death rituals are collectively called mixa gue'tu', or death mass.

I attended many mixa gue'tu' but one that particularly stands out was put on by Soledad, the cantinera, to commemorate the twenty-second anniversary of her mother's death. The fiesta was so large that the food preparations required the space of two neighbors' yards. Preparations began at dusk the evening before with the cooking of maize in huge iron kettles over open fires, to be made into hundreds of tortillas the following day. At 2:00 a.m. two oxen were slaughtered not twenty feet from my hammock and by daylight the beef was already cooking, the ox heads skinned, and the hides neatly folded and placed in the bed of the oxcart.

Over two hundred guests attended this mixa gue'tu' and about twenty women spent the entire day serving food to the steady stream of well-wishers.

Coming from American culture, where death is an almost completely taboo subject, I found it a refreshing change to be in a culture where death is treated so openly and where it enters everyday speech quite naturally and unconsciously in sayings like: "If God wills it, I will come tomorrow." Zapotecs remember and revere their dead in a way Americans do not, publicly and without embarrassment. Women wear mourning clothes for up to a year to honor deceased parents. Fresh flowers imported from Oaxaca are placed on graves twice a week for up to a year and at regular but less frequent intervals thereafter. People go to the cemetery to talk to missed loved ones. On one occasion I know of, sisters, cousins, friends, and the *novio* (fiance) of a young woman who died of tetanus at age twenty-three, held a birthday party in the cemetery on what would have been her 25th birthday anniversary.

In addition, there are the special holidays for the dead, called *Todos Santos* (All Saints' Day), celebrated all over Mexico. In the Isthmus, they celebrate the return of spirits not only on November 1 and 2 but again during the week preceding Easter. The November rites are centered on the house altars where special fruits, breads, flowers, beverages, and candles are set out on the household shrine to honor the spirits of dead relatives as they return to their old home. Neighbors and friends visit the houses of persons deceased during the previous year to pay respects to the deceased and leave an offering.

Easter week witnesses hundreds of Zapotec families spending the night at the graves of loved ones in the cemeteries. Families bring food, drink, flowers, and decorations to the graves and often hire musicians to play over them. Everyone talks, visits with neighbors, makes grave offerings, and "keeps a wake" for the night. Immense markets spring up outside the gates to the cemeteries during these evenings, selling everything people need for the occasion—food, drinks, cigarettes, candles, flowers and decorations—lending a carnival atmosphere to the scene. The residential areas of the towns are so deserted during these nights that thieves have been known to run rampant burglarizing houses.

Since weddings take place on Sundays, Monday mornings in the central markets often see processions of the mothers of Sunday's brides, each with her own entourage, passing through the aisles with baskets of red hibiscus and bags of red confetti. The flowers are given to women to wear in their hair and everyone's head is sprinkled with a handful of red confetti—red symbolizing the virginity of the bride married the day before and expressing a wish for her future fertility.

It is rare to see non-Zapotecs at fiestas in San Juan although summers may bring occasional foreign tourists who learn of a fiesta in El Centro and come out to join the festivities. I always dreaded the arrival of these foreigners, finding them an excruciating embarrassment. Although they would never think of attending a sacred occasion in their home country so attired, these insensitive and ignorant people often arrived wearing short shorts, halter tops, and Hawaiian shirts and proceeded to barge right into the dancing, making magnificent fools of themselves as the local people laughed at their indecent dress and witless behavior. The true meaning of "ugly American" became clear to me on several such occasions where I was an unwilling and embarrassed observer.

7
Viajeras

Efforts to establish rapport with some of the viajeras, women who traveled regularly to buy and sell in other markets, finally paid off when Chica informed me that one of her sisters-in-law was a viajera. Chica, acting as my palanca, arranged an introduction and Feliciana and I struck it off well from the start. After several weeks of coordinating schedules, we finally arranged for Chica and me to go with her to San Marcos, one end of her circuit only about twenty miles from San Juan. The trip would only take about three hours and we would stay two days and nights while Feli traded her goods for salted fish and shrimp, and I could observe and take notes. Chica would help me by answering questions and translating from Zapotec as needed, something Feli would be too busy to do. I offered to pay our traveling expenses—the bus fares, meals, and incidentals. We would carry our hammocks and sleep in the market.

Feli was about my age and had two teenage daughters to look after her household and cook for a younger brother and their father during Feli's weekly absences of four or five days and nights. She had been making her trading circuit almost every week for nearly twenty years. The family owned a small parcel of land that Feli's husband and son worked while the two daughters took care of the household. Feli's trading had made the family affluent enough to build a new, traditional house and to sponsor a patron saint's fiesta a few years earlier. The family was well respected.

Hearing we were going, Feli's neighbor, Tivi, asked if her seven-year-old daughter, Rita, could go along to buy some fish. An infant at home prevented Tivi from doing her own trading and the family needed some income to see them through this period.

The four of us—Chica, Feli, little Rita, and I—caught the noon bus to San Marcos. Maybe bus is too grand a word for the vehicle, a battered, faded green *urbano* without window panes. The ponderous monster ground to a halt in front of us under a frying noon sun and we all climbed aboard, Feli first supervising the loading of her ten or so heavy baskets and boxes. The slat seats were arranged around the edges of the bus, facing inward and leaving the entire middle section open for freight. The bus was nearly full and the freight area was already piled so high that passengers sitting on opposite sides of the bus had to crane their necks to see friends on the other side. Only the area around the driver remained free from freight but quickly filled with standing passengers.

The driver depressed the clutch, maneuvered the arthritic gearshift, and, after a moment's hesitation, a reluctant response came from our mechanical ox as it began its long, slow journey. We had traveled no more than half a mile when we made what was to be the first of multiple stops. The driver's helper (copilot and mechanic) jumped out of the bus clutching a large tin and dipped water from a mud hole beside the road, pouring it into the radiator. After the third such stop in as many kilometers it became evident that the radiator was leaking like a fishnet.

More than an hour into our journey we stopped at a tiny hamlet where most of the standing passengers deboarded, allowing the rest of us a little more breathing space. Hamlet women hawked tortillas to passengers through the paneless windows and women on the bus began to open certain of their bundles. It was lunchtime.

"Ay, Ciana, sell me a peach!" someone shouted. Ciana responded by untying the cloth covering over one of her baskets and digging out a handful of scrubby peaches the size of golf balls. Money began changing hands as passengers bought and sold. A jovial mood prevailed as women munched the food and fed their children.

As the hot afternoon wore on, babies and small children fell asleep and everyone became silent and lethargic, nodding off as the bus lurched and swayed over the rutted road. Soon only a trail remained, then a trackless, sandy littoral. The driver seemed to follow the trail more by scent than sight, finding his way unerringly across wide stretches of loose sand and great shallow salt water lagoons so wide the opposite side was barely discernible, emerging on the far side at the precise spot to pick up the track. Some five hours after leaving San Juan, thanks to the leaking radiator, we arrived at our destination as the sun slowly slid below the horizon.

Except for the church and several small municipal buildings, all structures in San Marcos had reed walls and thatched roofs. The streets were ankle-deep in sand. Men wearing strange pointed straw hats walked about here and there, all the while knotting fishnets from rolls of string tied to their belts. Women scurried through the streets in faded blue huipiles and nondescript long calico or old-style red wraparound skirts, some carrying enamel washbasins on their heads and others with baskets slung over their arms. Many women wore terrycloth bath towels wound around their heads like turbans.

The people of San Marcos speak a language entirely distinct from Zapotec, so trade between the two groups is conducted in a kind of pidgin Spanish. Between these very different peoples, Zapotecs and Huaves, an uneasy symbiotic relationship seems to have existed for centuries, the Huaves trading sea products to the Zapotecs in return for maize and other agricultural products difficult to grow on their sandy, saline land.

The bus stopped in front of the marketplace which consisted of two long narrow thatched roofs set end to end and supported by poles and crossbeams. As soon as we set foot in the sand, local women began crowding around Feli with basins of fish and shrimp.

"Who is your friend?" they asked, motioning toward me.

"Oh, she is a big buyer! Much money!" was Feli's matter-of-fact reply. Astonished upon hearing this, I wondered if I had missed some vital bit of information concerning my presence for I carried only enough cash to take care of our needs for a couple of days and perhaps meet some modest emergency.

"No, we won't buy now. Tomorrow we buy!" Feli shouted at the crowd around her.

One by one the women drifted away to make other deals. Chica and I walked over to the center of the main plaza to buy some sweet rolls and coffee for supper while Feli unpacked and arranged her merchandise. I confided to Chica my anxiety about money and the trade I was expected to undertake next morning.

"Oh, don't worry," she laughed. "That was only to get the women to come back early with the best quality items. That way they will bring everything they have to us first."

Only partially reassured, I momentarily considered ways I might avoid the dawn encounter altogether, but prospects were bleak.

Feli had brought peaches, apples, and onions, all purchased in Oaxaca the previous Saturday, and a couple of baskets of San Juan bananas. While we were buying the bread and coffee, Feli purchased two fresh fish from a local girl, asking her to take them home and cook them for us. The girl soon returned with the fried fish and fresh tortillas, and we ate our simple meal standing in Feli's market stall in the gathering dusk.

Chica and I strung our hammocks end-to-end between the posts which supported the roof. Since Feli had forgotten her hammock, Chica willingly lent hers to her sister-in-law and Chica and I, being less portly, doubled up in my hammock, our heads at opposite ends, feet to center. In minutes I was asleep.

Then like a bolt of thunder came: "Wake up, wake up, Bevita! Here is the night watchman. A *peso* for the velador!"

Stumbling from the hammock I began fumbling around in my duffle bag in search of a coin while the old night watchman waited patiently. His duties consisted of hanging a lantern here and there to discourage intruders and making some minimal efforts at sweeping the sandy floor clear of trash in return for a peso from each vendor.

We settled back into our hammocks. Chica, though, was restless and feared she was keeping me awake. Despite my protests, she moved to the sawhorse table covered with *pencas* (palm fronds with stems attached), staunchly claiming she was used to sleeping on hard, irregular surfaces.

Shuffling feet, swishing skirts, and low voices awakened me. In the half light of dawn I tried to orient myself. Feli's voice cleared my head.

"Wake up, Bevita! It's time to clear away the hammocks. We have to make room!"

I made my usual graceless exit from the hammock, rubbing the sleep from my eyes. Chica was already up, helping Feli unpack her goods and keep track of transactions. Like most Zapotec market women, Feli kept her accounts mentally. In the rush of heavy trading that was no mean trick.

As darkness lifted, I could see that the whole place was alive with local women waiting their turns to bargain with Feli and the other traders. Knowing that Chica was always pressed for money, I asked her if she did not want to buy some fish to resell in Oaxaca, offering to advance her the small amount I had with me. She declined. She had tried this business once, she said, only to have all her fish confiscated in Oaxaca because she had failed to obtain a resale permit for them. No, she wanted no more of that business.

Rapid trading made it impossible for me to keep track of individual transactions, and there proved to be no way to keep account of transactions made by trade, for example, so many apples for a handful of fish. Each transaction was unique and the rapidity with which they were accomplished was dizzying to watch. In the end I had to be content with estimates of the day's purchases made by noting the size of the containers and their contents.

Feli was an accomplished trader. When the local women told her they needed maize instead of fruit, she expressed amazement that they were passing up the opportunity of the season by not trading for her fruit because fruits were filled with vitamins, marvelous for curing illnesses. Someone asked her what apples cured and she replied without a moment's hesitation that they cured colds and bronchial ailments.

"Just cook them in a little water, add cinnamon and drink them." A few women traded their fish for a handful of vitamin-packed, though wormy, apples.

By mid-morning, activity had slowed enough so that we could go over to the main plaza for breakfast—coffee and sweet bread. Seven-year-old Rita did no active trading but played in the sand drawing figures with a stick or idling about watching Feli trade. Through the long, hot day the child remained quietly absorbed in her play, not once bothering her elders with complaints of boredom, hunger, or thirst. Now and then Feli bought a batch of fish on Rita's behalf and put them aside for the little girl to take home.

Chica looked tired. As the day wore on she became quiet, weary, and obviously uncomfortable and finally admitted that she felt ill and wanted to go home. Consulting with Feli, it was agreed that Chica and I should return to San Juan while Feli and Rita stayed over to finish their buying the following day as planned. They would send their day's purchases back with us: three baskets of turtle eggs, a live sheep, and several containers of salted fish. We would have to get them off the truck and see that they were delivered to Feli's home when we arrived in San Juan.

Our return vehicle, this time a *redila* (stock truck with high slat sides and no top) arrived. Already several people had scrambled aboard when Chica grabbed my hand and pulled me up the ladder, leading me to the front of the truck just in back of the cab where a covered tool chest served as the only seat, large enough to accommodate only two or three persons. Pushing aside an empty gunnysack, she told me to sit down and stay there so that I would not lose the spot. Chica then went back to the loading end and helped load our cargo, including the sheep. A goat near me was not happy at his unfamiliar surroundings and began to protest, bleating and switching his rear end nervously from side to side in the small space he had perilously near my legs.

Loud voices and a commotion at the loading end drew my attention. Chica and an enormous Zapotec woman I did not recognize were exchanging angry words. Suddenly the woman was bulldozing her way over the freight, animals, and people toward where I sat, without a pause in her steady stream of Zapotec expletives. The woman broke through the last entanglement of boxes, baskets, goats, sheep, turkeys, and passengers, and loomed over me like a storm cloud about to rain. Too late I realized Chica had seated me in the place this woman had reserved for herself.

"Don't move! Don't move! She has no right to that seat!" Chica shouted at me just as the woman began to sit down.

Rights or no rights, instincts of self-preservation prevailed. I drew my legs up under me and turned sideways just as the woman's full weight struck me a glancing blow on the left thigh. Somehow I slipped from under descending doom to freedom. Although squeezed unpleasantly between the side of the truck and my angry neighbor, I felt lucky to have survived without injury. In the semi-fetal position I had defensively assumed I was able to endure the four-hour journey home with my back turned toward my still outraged seatmate.

This fortuitous turn of events for me failed to quell the argument; Chica and her furious opponent continued to shout bitter insults at one another. Twice on the homeward journey, the quarrel became so heated that the driver stopped the truck, climbed out of the cab and came back to threaten: "*Señoras*! *Señoras*! If you do not stop this argument immediately I will put you both out right here and you can walk home." The improbability of a lone, average-sized man dislodging an angry Zapotec woman built like a Sumo wrestler seemed to occur neither to the driver nor the combatants. His threat served to cool the verbal battle temporarily as each participant mulled over the prospects of a lengthy walk in the dark.

All during the long trip home Chica stood staunchly in her corner at the very back of the truck, pale and morose. Dust from the rear wheels swirled around her and the other unfortunate rear passengers. She had told me she was ill, and I thought she was probably suffering from motion sickness as well, just as she had on the trip to Oaxaca. I hoped she could feel my empathy as she stood sullen and pathetic, stubborn to the end. I wanted desperately to offer up my little space, but even if there had been a way to do so, she would have refused. She had saved the seat for me and I would have to occupy it. So the only gesture of sympathy which seemed appropriate was to remain where I was, pretending to be unaware that I was the cause of the bitter exchange. Days later, when I attempted to pry the details of the quarrel from her all she would say was: "Oh, that ugly woman! Her vagina is completely worthless!"

A couple of weeks passed before I was able to complete the other half of Feli's trade route, taking salted fish to Oaxaca. This time, Feli, her trading partner Ana, and I boarded the midnight second-class bus in El Centro and found it already nearly full. Feli and Ana managed to secure seats. I, being neither as clever nor as fast as they, ended up sitting on the floor at the back of the bus until several people deboarded about two hours into the journey. By this time Feli and Ana were already sleeping soundly. Although I tried, sleep was impossible as the bus slowly climbed up the mountains, the mostly snoring passengers shifting from side to side as we rounded curve after curve after curve.

We arrived in Oaxaca at dawn. Feli and Ana hired a porter to carry their many boxes and bundles to the market by wheelbarrow, where Feli and I found a place on the street of fish traders and settled down on the curb to wait for customers. Ana took up a similar position on the opposite side of the street. We bought breakfast from women passing by with coffee, tacos, and other snacks. Sales were very slow so I had little trouble keeping track of them for my notes. At midmorning Feli left me in charge and disappeared up the street, soon returning with a wholesale buyer who purchased all her fish. I rejoiced. We would soon be on our way home! But after a few minutes when I noticed no move on Feli's part to begin packing up her empty containers I asked when we would be going to the bus station.

"Ay, no, Bevita! We can't go home until this evening. We must wait until late in the day to make our purchases at the best prices."

Not long after that discouraging news, I told Feli I was going to see if I could rent a room at a nearby hotel to nap in for a few hours, having spent a sleepless night on the bus. She insisted that there was no need for that. Her godchild who was attending medical school had a room nearby and would be happy to let me rest there for a few hours. She left to see about the room and returned shortly with her godchild, Rogelio, in tow.

After showing me to his room, Rogelio left and I found myself alone in a small cell of a room in an ancient colonial building. Except for the ceiling which was a good sixteen feet high, the room would have seemed as cramped as a doghouse. The only window was a small circle near the timbered ceiling which let in a tiny cylinder of light. Furnishings were a small table, a crude wood chair, and a burlap-covered cot similar to ones I had seen in San Juan. It strained my imagination to think of myself trying to study for a medical degree in this dark and bleak convent-like cubicle.

It was late afternoon when I awoke, rested but hungry, to rejoin Feli and Ana. Among their purchases made while I was sleeping were scrubby apples and peaches, multiple bundles of flowers that were a little the worse for the day's wear but would be welcome in San Juan for the Sunday morning cemetery trade and a few other items. We walked back to the bus station while a porter hauled their freight alongside in a wheelbarrow.

Boarding the bus after the big Saturday market in Oaxaca takes both cunning and practice. We had about thirty minutes to plan our strategy. I was to carry all their money, contained in two cloth bags, which I dutifully tucked into my shoulder bag. Even though reasons were given, I never learned the true reasons why the role of money-carrier was invariably relegated to me. Was it because would-be pickpockets would not suspect the gringa to be carrying the viajeras' day's receipts or was it because they reasoned that if I lost the money I would be good for it?

The bus-boarding strategy called for Ana, a ninety-pound sylph, to wait at the street entrance to the bus terminal and board the empty bus as the door automatically cracked open a few inches when the driver applied the brake to turn in. Being knife-thin she could slip through that cracked door easily. Ana would then secure the best double seat in the empty bus. I was to elbow my way mercilessly to the front of the waiting crowd to be one of the first few on the bus when it began loading, thus securing my own seat.

"Don't be polite!" Feli warned. "You must push and shove your way right through the crowd!"

Ana, meanwhile, would open a window from inside to receive some of their freight bundles while Feli remained outside, passing the packages through the window and overseeing the porter loading their larger items on the top of the bus. At the last minute Feli would board to claim her seat saved by Ana. They were nervous that I would bungle my part, not an unreasonable assumption, and be left standing behind with the money to await another bus many hours later.

"Now, Bevita, do you know what you are to do?"

"Yes," I said, "I think so."

"Well, just to be sure let's go over it again," Feli insisted. We reviewed every move aloud.

When the bus arrived the plan proceeded without a hitch. Somehow I managed to be the third person on the bus, wading ruthlessly through the jam of waiting and determined passengers. Perhaps people were so surprised at such an aggressive gringa that they forgot to stand their ground as I shoved and elbowed to the front.

With the three of us comfortably seated while the aisles were jammed with standing passengers, we settled down for the long ride home. Ana had cleverly maneuvered herself into my seat, shared with a rather small young man, and I ended up sharing with Feli, only later understanding Ana's deft seat switch. Feli was asleep in minutes, snoring soundly. At every one of the road's over seven hundred curves (yes, I counted them) Feli's limp, portly form shifted alternately onto me or against the window. The night proved to be every bit as long as the previous one, my only entertainment being the chorus of snoring passengers and the bus driver's inexplicable and repeated practice of running without headlights down the sinuous mountain road for minutes on end.

8

Viajeras Too

In fieldwork, opportunities, like San Juan *sancudos* (mosquitoes), come in swarms. Within a week after the trip to Oaxaca with Feli and Ana, another trip I had been working on for months suddenly opened up. My comadre Alberta's elder sister, Carlota, had been a viajera for many years. We had met several times and she was willing to take me along on one of her trips. For the past year or so she had been going to a big hydroelectric construction site in the state of Chiapas, about 350 miles from San Juan, doing a brisk business in the boom town of La Laguna which had sprung up in the wilderness around the project.

Carlota's strategy was to be at La Laguna with a full inventory on the semi-monthly project paydays, spending seven to ten days there, then returning to the Isthmus to replenish her stock before the next payday. Our joint trip had been delayed again and again because Carlota was caring for her bedridden, dying mother and had not been able to make her regular schedule in the last few months. When her mother seemed a little better she decided suddenly to go because she desperately needed income and because I was willing to drive the pick-up and pay our travel expenses.

Several weeks before when I had told my comadre Jonsa of my plan to go with Carlota, Comadre Jonsa had tried to dissuade me, saying that Carlota was a "loose woman," and Jonsa worried about my welfare in such company. I attributed the report of negative character to the fact that Carlota was about forty-five years old, had been single for at least fifteen years and traveled constantly. She seemed to me to be a respectable and refined woman. So when this opportunity knocked, I jumped to answer.

The timing of the trip could not have been worse for me personally. Although I had managed to work around a periodic health problem (menorrhagia) for several years, the morning we left San Juan found me facing the situation square on. Common sense told me to postpone the trip. My ethnographer's soul said go, no matter what, or I may never have another chance. I went.

A prescription painkiller brought from home made it possible to function but the prospect of sitting long hours in the driver's seat without a break and with no restroom facilities along the way gave me pause. I really wondered how I would manage. Before we got under way I explained the dilemma to Carlota who had a solution. When it became necessary, she said, we could just stop by the side of the highway and she would hold her long full skirts around me to make a tent while I changed clothing.

We drove to Xochitlan where she purchased most of her goods at favorable prices. While we drove that short thirty kilometers, she asked me to loan her a thousand pesos just for the duration of the trip. Always reluctant to loan money, I explained that I had not brought a great amount of cash with me, but she promised to repay me in La Laguna as soon as she sold enough merchandise to raise the repayment. I knew from her sister that Carlota had spent most of her assets—even to her jewelry and clothing—caring for her mother and at the same time losing months of work. I loaned her the money. With the newly acquired cash, she loaded up the pick-up with salted shrimp, sweet bread, totopos, apricots, green mangoes, cheese, raw sugar, nuts, tamarind seeds, sour cream, and brooms. She also carried a small cache of gold jewelry on consignment from a goldsmith in Xochitlan. The jewelry case she promptly entrusted to me. By now I was accustomed to my role as carrier of valuables and accepted the jewelry as part of my job. I was thankful that the filled pick-up did not seem over-loaded weight-wise, recalling the earlier hauling trip with Chica's mangoes.

Carlota and I struck it off well from the start. She was in a euphoric mood to be going on a selling trip that would not cost her anything. Carlota had travelled over many parts of Mexico and was curious about my work and life in the United States. She was still a beauty, seemed a perfect lady, spoke good Spanish, did not use street language, and dressed well in the last of her clothes and jewelry. She certainly did not fit my preconceived idea of what a prostitute would be like. If she was a "loose woman" as Comadre Jonsa had indicated, Carlota carried it off with admirable class and discretion. By the time we had traveled several hours I had learned a good deal about why she became a viajera and her tragic past.

At sixteen her family had forced her to marry a young man who had grabbed her in the street and tried to rape her, possibly succeeding. In those days, that was considered a "marriage by robbing" and although she protested she had never seen him before, her relatives believed the worst, that she was lying and had been secretly meeting him. Only her mother believed that Carlota was an innocent victim and fought for her daughter, but the extended family prevailed.

The marriage was a disaster. The man turned out to be as violent as his first actions indicated. He beat her and mistreated her continually. Within a year she produced a son who died before he was two years old. Divorce was very shameful back then (around 1940) and Carlota stuck with the marriage for fourteen incredibly agonizing years, mainly because the man threatened to kill her and her mother if she left. When she did leave, lucky to get away alive, she hid in her mother's house. The husband burned and otherwise destroyed all her clothing and tried to set fire to her mother's house. She managed to escape to Mexico City, spending several years moving around from place to place to throw her husband-pursuer off track. The only work she knew was market-selling, learned in her mother's market stall as a girl. So that was how she became a viajera. After some years she learned that her husband had been imprisoned for murder and she returned to her mother's house, continuing her selling journeys for a livelihood. Because her mother believed in her and supported her when no one else would, any sacrifice she had to make now for her mother could never repay the debt, Carlota declared.

In midafternoon we stopped at the last town on the highway before our turn-off onto an unimproved road to the project. Carlota had relatives here who ran a little cafe and with whom she left items on her way home, to be picked up on return. The Gulf Coast heat and humidity was even more debilitating than that of the Isthmus. I had no appetite but Carlota insisted that we both eat because there would be nothing in La Laguna when we arrived after the market closed. The little cafe was filthy with flies, grease, dirty dishes, and clutter.

The usual mangy dogs scavenged under the table around our feet as I tried to swallow a little of the liver and vegetable stew. Carlota ate hers with relish but, even in the name of good manners, I could only get down a few spoonfuls. When the cafe owner/chef/waitress noticed that I could eat no more she unceremoniously picked up my plate and scraped it back into the pot from whence it came. I made a mental note not to eat here on our return even if Carlota did.

The unimproved road was just that; dirt and rocks, gigantic chuckholes and outright gullies. It worsened as we climbed higher and higher into the mountains. We arrived at La Laguna well after dark. The lights were still on in the market shed so Carlota went to look for someone to help her unload. Although we had stopped once for me to change clothes along the roadside, I was again sitting in a pool of blood, my clothing soaked through and through from the hours of driving without respite. People crowded around the pick-up, curious to see a gringa in this isolated place and, as always, amazed that a woman was driving a truck. Carlota and I had planned that, to avoid embarrassment, I would wait in the truck until she had unloaded her goods, then we would drive the two blocks to her quarters where I could get out and enter her room in the dark without observation.

Carlota shared a windowless cubicle in a thrown-together wood building with four other viajeras. Since her San Juan roommate was gone, I would be able to set up my camp cot in her space.

The roommates were all absent when we arrived, the quarters dark. Once inside, Carlota groped around in the blackness until she found a candle and matches. Glancing around in the dim candlelight I was appalled by the clutter and lack of space. Five women lived intermittently, sometimes for weeks on end, in this tiny room I judged to be about twelve feet square. A board partition of sorts reaching to about six inches from the low ceiling separated our cubicle from the others on either side. One could see through the half-inch cracks between the boards without difficulty when the lamps were lit. Our neighbor on the one side was a lively cantina, and on the other was a family with several small children. There was no running water in the room but Carlota explained that a public bathroom was about a block up the street and she would take me there after I washed up and changed clothes. She dipped some water into a basin from an uncovered oil barrel in the corner. Past camping trips in California's Sierras came to mind, the campgrounds with clean running water, flush toilets, and showers. We called *that* roughing it, I mused.

To clear a space for my cot we had to pile cartons, baskets, cooking pans, and clothing on the table, the only visible furniture in the room. It was well after 11:00 p.m. when we finally settled down for the night. Some hours later I was awakened by the sound of shuffling pans. Someone had lit a candle and was busily working in the corner near the water barrel.

"*Quien*?" I inquired.

"It's I, making the *arroz con leche*," a woman's voice responded. I went back to sleep.

By 6:00 a.m. Carlota was up and dressed and had taken down her hammock when she called me.

"Get up, get up, Bevita! We have to put your cot away and make room in here."

Except for a kerosene lamp on the table the room was still pitch dark although I could see through the cracks in the walls it was

Room shared by five Isthmus Viajeras

beginning to get light outside. The room, it turned out, was eternally dark even on the brightest day because it was windowless.

When the market opened at 7:00 a.m., we were there waiting to start the day. I helped Carlota unpack and store some of the foods we had brought as the customers began to stream through the aisles buying breakfast items. My fieldwork tasks were to note items and the prices of the things Carlota sold each day. At the end of a week I would have a record of her gross sales from which I could calculate, fairly accurately, her net profits by deducting the cost of the goods we bought in Xochitlan and allowing for the traveling and shipping expenses which she normally would have had. Since Zapotec marketers do not keep written records, most have only vague ideas of what their net income is. Mark-ups are a percentage added to the cost of the item, the percentage determined by competition and custom.

Carlota's cousin, Rosario, a middle-aged woman with a son she was putting through college, did business in the next market stall and the two women cooperated by watching each other's stalls and by cooking and eating together. As is the custom everywhere in Mexico, market women, working often twelve or more hours per day, take most of their meals on the job. A lull after the first rush of customers gave Carlota time to buy what we needed for breakfast from other vendors while Rosario boiled coffee on a small brazier. We ate standing at the counter, I keeping my records while Carlota waited on customers.

This meal and all the others we had the week I stayed with Carlota in the market were tasty and nutritious. Most Zapotec women are incredibly good cooks even with the limited ingredients with which they sometimes have to cook. Notwithstanding the roadside cafe we had stopped at on our trip, Zapotec women are generally very discerning about food. If their eyes and noses tell them it is anything but the freshest, it goes to the pigs or the dog. They are all aware of occasional episodes of food poisoning, sometimes fatal, due to careless handling of food. At home in San Juan my friends would warn me sometimes not to buy cooked food from certain vendors because they were known to sell reheated food kept overnight.

At the next lull we had in business, Carlota took me around the small market to introduce me to the other sellers. About half of the twenty or so stalls were run by Isthmus women, while some of the others were operated by men from other areas. Our roommate who was making the rice gruel in the middle of the night proved to be a large woman named Dolores.

Dolores, also from the Isthmus, was a happy woman with a pleasant face, a widow with one son whom she was putting through medical school. She had been living and selling here for several years, getting up at 2:00 a.m. each morning to make the arroz con leche which she sold to construction workers in front of the market seven days a week, beginning before dawn. During the day she sold fruit and other food items in her market stall until the market closed at 8:00 p.m. She never took a siesta, she said, and survived on about five hours of sleep per night year after year.

It was already dark when the market closed. Without lights in our room there was no "after work" life. We took showers at the public baths, set up the cot and hammocks and dropped off to sleep.

The remaining days in La Laguna were much like the first except that by the third day the presence of such an exotic creature as I had attracted a determined and unwelcome suitor. The man began coming by our market stall at regular intervals, trying to find out my name and inviting me for a "drink." He appeared to be an office worker but, since I did not speak to him following the advice of Carlota and Rosario, I never discovered who he was or what he did.

Taking my cue from Zapotec women's proper etiquette in such encounters, I looked straight through this person with arms folded across my chest and said nothing. To Isthmus men this formidable stance conveys the message that their attentions are unwelcome. Not so for this man who seemed to be from somewhere else. He began bringing gifts—first a rose, then a bottle of wine. I neither accepted nor acknowledged them. The second day the man had the nerve to follow me to the bathroom, trying all the while to get a response from me. I was growing weary of his game and complained to Carlota about the bathroom incident. Not to worry, she said, she and Rosario would handle him. Their solution was to pay two small girls a few centavos to stand at each of the two entrances to the market and signal us when the man approached. At the signal, I ducked behind the counter while Carlota and Rosario told him I had left. He soon gave up. When I thought about Comadre Jonsa's worries that I would not be in good company, I was much amused and wondered how I could ever be better protected from bad influences than I was by Carlota and Rosario.

On Saturday night Carlota produced from among her goods a little jug of mezcal and the three roommates and I spent a couple of hours in our dark little cubicle polishing it off, visiting, and telling jokes and stories. Two other Isthmus women and a young man who was the novio of one joined us. The cantina next door was alive with activity. Long after our guests had left and all was quiet, I lay wide-eyed, staring at the dark ceiling while rats played their rat games along the rafters above my cot.

Sunday, the biggest day of the market, was very busy because this is the day many country people come in, traveling long distances on foot. Unlike the dam workers, they had no regularly paying jobs or steady source of income and therefore had very little money. They would want to buy a peso's worth of salted shrimp or cheese, scarcely more than a taste. Carlota had certain quantity limits on her merchandise and would not sell less than two pesos worth of shrimp or cheese. In spite of much pleading by the poor country folks, she would never relax her rules. After they left without their purchase, though, she would express her sympathy for them and their poverty-stricken lives. It took determination to maintain one's very small margin of profit in the competitive and small-scale business of market-selling. If Carlota relented, she would be swamped by requests for these minimal quantities. One could easily end up losing money and in the end, become as destitute as those unfortunate country folk.

By early Sunday afternoon, Romero, a man from the Isthmus who sold candy from a cart on the streets (a very unusual occupation for a Zapotec man and one he would never do in his own home region), came into the market talking loudly and cursing. We had met and talked before because the niece of our roommate Dolores, who also sold in the market, lived with him. Now in his drunken state he headed straight for our stall and began berating me for the role of the United States in the Vietnam war! However much I tried to tell him that I agreed with much of what he said, he didn't hear a word. His hostility grew until Rosario took me by the arm and asked me to walk her to the bathroom. We stayed away until we felt Romero had left. He returned several times during the afternoon and evening but our two posted guards, now alert to the new threat, signaled each time and I ducked behind the counter.

That night and the following night, Dolores slept in the quarters of her niece, Marga, to protect her from the possible abuse of the drunken and violent Romero. This did not surprise me. I had found that female Zapotec relatives regularly rally around a woman threatened by a drunken husband or novio, keeping her under their protection until the danger has passed. This was another instance of women as peacekeepers to add to my growing list of examples of such behavior.

We stayed eight days in La Laguna and the records I collected about Carlota's market business completed another link in the knowledge I was gaining about market vendors' earnings, expenses, and lifestyles. I returned to San Juan with a new appreciation of the skills and energy one must have to be a successful viajera and of the hardships the women endure in their travels.

9

Doña Lucia

After I returned from the trip to La Laguna, Chica and I continued to work together on the questionnaire interviews, doing one or two a week. I had no trouble filling the time between interviews with the several other field sub-projects I was always working on. Just spending time talking with people about the past, about their present lives and problems, and listening to people talk with each other, were helping me gain insight into the culture and the people.

One of the people I began spending a good deal of time with was Chica's mother, Doña Lucia. Lucia was a tiny wraith, less than five feet tall and weighing about eighty-five pounds. Although she was only sixty, not old by American standards, her cheeks were sunken under prominent cheekbones, her arms delicate as river reeds, and she was nearly toothless. Worse, Lucia suffered wracking seizures of coughing, and she occasionally spat blood. Don't worry, she assured me, it was not tuberculosis but something connected with her diabetes. She also suffered recurring bouts of chills and fever, perhaps malaria, and many days found her too weak to rise from the hammock. But even in this state of declining health it was apparent that she had been a beauty in younger days. Wisps of her snowy white hair still curled prettily around her face and behind her ears even as she tried to control it by wetting it and pulling it into tight braids. When she was strong enough, Doña Lucia loved to talk and reminisce, and her mind was as sharp as her appetite was dull.

Doña Lucia was a gold mine of knowledge about San Juan and its residents. We talked about the "olden days," and she filled in my crude house-count census. She had spent all of her sixty years in San Juan and she knew a great many of the more than seven thousand residents. From memory while lying in her hammock she had given me the names, approximate ages, kin relations, and occupations of the residents of nearly two hundred households. Later when I was able to check her list against the official school census I found she was often the more accurate of the two.

Doña Lucia looked forward to our chats. Time hung heavy on her hands as her physical condition grew progressively weaker. She now spent most of her time in the hammock or lying on a western-style bed her son had purchased to give her respite from the hammock now and then. Talking and listening were the only ways she had of passing the time, since she could neither read nor write. As a key informant, Doña Lucia was just about perfect. She took great pride in being accurate in what she said, exhibiting little patience with my rechecking items she had already covered. As we were taught to do in graduate school, it was my practice to bring up the same question again after three or four days had elapsed if I had some reason to doubt my understanding or her memory.

"But we already talked about that!" she would exclaim. "Don't you remember?"

I would explain that I thought perhaps I had not understood correctly the first time. I knew that questioning her memory would be taken as an insult, something to be avoided at all cost. She always cooperated by repeating, but not without letting me know that I should try harder to get these things straight the first time.

Collecting life histories is a part of many ethnographic field projects because they can provide valuable information about the past and the changes which have occurred during a person's lifetime and how those changes were perceived and dealt with by the individual. Life histories are also fun to collect because the narrator is an older person with a long life history and usually enjoys the experience of telling someone about their life. I broached the subject with Doña Lucia who loved to relate vignettes of her life. I told her I wanted to write down her life for my book because it was so interesting and at the same time it could teach students who read the book about life here in San Juan and what it was like in earlier days. She agreed and, sick as she was, I think she found the telling of her life history as enjoyable an experience as I did.

"The town has grown since I was a girl," began Doña Lucia, responding to my question. "Then there were less streets and the streets were shorter. More houses were just of reeds instead of adobe. At the other end of San Juan where there are houses now there were fields then and there were no houses at all on the hill.

"There were seven children in our family. I was about in the middle, two younger than I there were. Now they are all gone except my two brothers and me. Long ago my mother died. She went to the river to bathe one day and just fell dead. My father lived to be a very old man, in his eighties when he died about—let's see, it was when Angela (a grandchild) was a baby so it must have been six years ago. Yes, there were seven of us in our family, but people said my father really had nineteen children by various women. That's what they said but I don't know.

"When I was about ten, Tia Tina, my father's sister, who lived in El Centro, became concerned because we were not attending school. My father and his brothers and sisters could all read and write. Auntie decided we must go to school. She bought our slates and books and enrolled my brother and me in the school.

"I didn't like school at all. It was miserable, I tell you. The children, some of them big boys, made the teacher's work a martyrdom. Nobody understood a word of the lessons because the teacher was speaking Spanish and we understood only Zapotec. It was a tremendous bore. To break the monotony the boys would fight right in the classroom, in front of the teacher. Everybody talked and shouted among themselves in Zapotec while the 'maestro' droned on and on in Spanish, giving the lessons.

"When we could endure it no longer we devised a plan. Each morning I would don my school huipil and skirt and take my slate and lunch, but I did not go to school. Instead my brother and I and some other children would head for the river. There were a great many children who were not enrolled in school or who were enrolled but seldom attended so we had plenty of company. The trees and bushes along the river made it easy to stay out of sight and with so many children it was hard to tell one from another from a distance. Once at the river I would take off my school clothes and lay them under a bush. We would play all day long in the river, then quickly dress and go home again when we saw the other children coming from

Doña Lucia

school. I broke so many slates my aunt became very angry but she kept replacing them. We practiced this ruse for almost a whole term, only going to school now and then.

"At the end of the term my father asked me to demonstrate what I had learned. Ah, then I knew the game was up! I could not even write my name. He asked me to recite the numbers. Of course, I could not do that either. I had not learned one thing! 'All right, young lady,' said my father, 'you have learned nothing in school so you will learn at home.' And he saw to it that I did—but not reading, writing, and numbers. I learned to make cheese, to sew, to make tortillas, to make candles, and to cook. After that, I never had a moment to play. My life became just work, work, work.

"I was twenty-two when I came to this house. Then Sole's house was the only house and what is now our place was a part of their house site. Sole's grandmother and Inocencio's mother were sisters. When I came here they were widows living in that house together. Inocencio had been away from San Juan for many years, maybe ten or more. He was years older than I and I did not know him before he left, being only a small girl. He came back one day, and a few months later I told my father I wanted to go live with Censo. My father was furious! 'If you are crazy enough to go live with that *viejo* (old man) I have no sympathy for you!' I was very fond of my father but I went anyway. Censo had been to your country, you know, and could speak your language. I think he had been in some placed called Texas for a long time. He worked for the railroad there.

"Well, so I came to live in this place. Censo partitioned off the back part of the lot for us. There was no street between this place and Soledad's then. On this back part of the lot there was only a very small *choza* (reed hut) right over there where the bathroom is now, and that is where we lived for a long time. Censo didn't drink in those days. Well, yes, he drank but not like later after Geronimo became ill.

"In those days we raised sugar cane. Did you know that all the milpa area used to be sugar cane? No, no, there was always maize but there was sugar cane instead of bananas and sesame as we have now, you understand. Anyway, we raised sugar cane and the prices were good. I sold the cane and other things we raised and collected the money for them the same as I do now with the milk. I longed for a respectable house instead of that poor little reed shack and, since I took in the money from the sugar cane, I could put away a few pesos regularly toward my house. I didn't tell Censo or anybody because I knew he would spend the money in the cantinas. No, I kept it a secret, hiding the money in an *olla* (large clay pot) I had buried in the corner over there where the lemon tree is now.

"At last the olla was full and I decided to count the pesos and see if I had enough to order some of the material for the house. By this time I had three children—Chica, Magda, and Sefa, just a babe in arms. Chica, the oldest, was still small, about four years old. One morning after Censo left for the milpa I told Chica we were going to count the money and not to tell a word about it to her papa.

"I dug up the olla and spread the pesos out in the *batea* (wooden tub) to count them. Then, Ay, Dios mio! I heard Censo coming back! What was I to do? I squatted in the tub and spread my skirt over the money. 'What are you doing sitting there in that batea?' he asked. 'Oh, I am just getting ready to bathe,' I lied, trying to act as calm and natural as I could. My heart was pounding though! He didn't say anything, just picked up his machete, the reason he had returned, and left. I waited a long time, sitting there in that batea. Then when I was sure he was gone to the milpa I counted the money, and I had a little over two thousand pesos. I couldn't believe it! Two thousand pesos!

That very same day I ordered some bricks. I ordered them delivered just a few at a time and it was quite a while before Censo noticed the pile growing over in the corner because they were behind that big rock. When he noticed, we had a big fight. He said I had stolen the money from him. Chica, being just a little girl, couldn't keep the secret and told him where I had hidden the money. He called me a thief! He was really angry, cursing and raging. But his mother took my part. 'Huh!' she said, 'so she stole the money from you so she would have a house for your children. What kind of robbery is that?' He knew he was defeated then. He let the matter drop, and I continued with my plans for the house.

"Yes," continued Doña Lucia, answering my question, "Censo's mother always took my part. Not long after Censo discovered my plan to build a real house, I know when it was because Sefa was still quite small, Censo told me he had another woman, a cantinera in Xochitlan, and he wanted to go live with her. We fought about that for a long time. He would be gone for days, then come home. Finally his mother and I devised a plan whereby whenever he came past a neighbor's house, the neighbor would notify us and the children and I would quickly hide in his mother's house. She would tell him we were gone, she didn't know where. The girls were little and it wasn't hard to conceal ourselves for a short while. He did not come often and he never stayed long. We played that game for quite a while. Then one day when he came I said I was back but I would stay only if he quit seeing the cantinera. We finally came to an agreement because he didn't want me to leave and take the children. He gave up the cantinera as far as I could tell and we got along better after that.

"When Ramon (fourth child) was born, we had about half of this part of the house (main room) built. Did I ever tell you about when Ramon was born?" With that, Doña Lucia was off on another tale of her life story.

"Doña Lucia," I ventured, after a couple of sessions. "Your life is so interesting I want to write it all down accurately but you know I can't get every word so why don't I bring the tape recorder when we talk?" I had approached the same subject once or twice before but now I thought perhaps she would be more comfortable since she knew me better. She agreed, and I suggested that we begin with the tape recorder next day.

The next morning Doña Lucia was not feeling well. She had not slept at all, she said, just worrying about talking into that machine. She was afraid. I told her not to worry, we would not use it. I never mentioned the tape recorder again. By listening carefully, only jotting a note now and then so I could later recall the sequence when I wrote my notes a few hours later, we got along perfectly well without the tape recorder. By writing up the notes immediately after a session, which I was usually able to do, I found I could recall her account nearly word for word.

"Now where were we yesterday?" she asked, when she was at ease again.

"You were going to tell me about when Ramon was born," I reminded her after consulting my notes.

"Oh, yes, now I remember. Yes, when Chica was about six Ramon was born. My children are all about two years apart. I remember I got very sick and weak and I just seemed to get worse and worse.

One day I went over and laid down on the big rock in the corner and I said to Censo 'You had better send for the *curandera* (native curer) because I am very sick. I think I am going to die.'

"When the curandera came she looked right into my eyes close up and then she said, 'Huh, huh, huh! Why didn't you tell me you were in *estado*?' 'I'm pregnant?' I asked, surprised. 'Of course,' she said, looking straight into my eyes again, 'and this time you are going to have a son!' 'A son!' Censo shouted. Since we had three girls, he wanted a son very much. 'If it's a boy we will have a big fiesta the day he is born and you (the curandera) will be invited.' And that is just what happened.

"When Ramon was born his father said, 'Yes, yes! We must make a fiesta right away!' He bought three chickens and the neighbor women came in to prepare the fiesta. He sent for the curandera and invited many other people. They had to prepare *twelve* chickens so many people came to celebrate the birth of my son! No, I didn't take part. I was too tired. I said, 'Have a good time, enjoy yourselves. I will just rest here on the *petate* (sleeping mat) with my son.'

" 'Now you have a son to take care of you in your old age,' Censo said. 'He will finish this house.' And that is precisely what occurred. Ramon finished this room when he grew up and then added the other rooms and kept making improvements. He is still building this house."

Over the weeks we continued with Doña Lucia's life history interviews as time and her health permitted. Doña Lucia was a natural storyteller, using gestures and expressive words to convey the drama of her life. And, as with most lives in San Juan, hers had been filled with dramatic and wrenching events. The long illness and death of her second son, Geronimo, and the sudden death of a three-year-old daughter, then the death of her husband, Censo, and the illness of her youngest daughter, Faustina.

"I have seen many difficult days, many times when it seemed that misfortune would always be with us. I have told you about Geronimo and all the years he was sick but did you know that my little daughter, younger than Geronimo, died when she was just three years old? Her name? Eulalia was her name. She took sick suddenly and died from fever not long before Faustina was born. Yes, I had seven children, five girls and two boys, and only five lived to grow up. Sefa may as well be dead. We have not heard from her in years. She married a man from Mexico City, you know. Once she came home with three little ones for a visit but she and her brother quarreled and she never returned. I heard roundabout that she lives in the north and has many children.

"Geronimo was sick for more than three years. It came on so suddenly too. One day on his way to school he fell down in the street and he could not get up. He never walked again but just grew worse and worse."

I guessed that Geronimo, about age twelve, had been a victim of poliomyelitis because he became paralyzed, but Doña Lucia did not know what his illness was called.

"Censo took Geronimo to doctors in Oaxaca, doctors in Mexico City, but nothing helped. Censo sold everything we had except the house and two small pieces of land to raise money for doctors. Geronimo was the most intelligent of all my children. Even though he could not walk, there was nothing wrong with his brain. We did his lessons at home, his father teaching him. When he died he was only fifteen years old. After that, Censo was never the same, he was never sober." Doña Lucia paused, remembering, then continued.

"Yes, after Geronimo died, Censo drank himself to death. But although he was a borracho in those years, my husband never mistreated me or the children. Not once did he ever raise a hand to us, God rest his soul.

"After Censo died (about 1956), Faustina took ill. Just a few months after her father died, Faustina, about twelve or thirteen years old, began to lose her appetite, to lose weight. She would cry for hours for no reason and she was afraid. She could not sleep at night. We could not find anything wrong with her. We tried several curers. Then I hired a man curer. He said a neighbor was bewitching Faustina and he advised us to have the house and lot cured, but to be very careful not to let the *bruja* (witch) who had placed the curse know so that she would not make stronger medicine. So he cured this place.

"See that patched spot beneath the other hammock there? That's where Faustina slept so we made a hole there in the floor and he cured that spot by burying the chiles and things there. Then he placed similar magical items in the niches we made in the walls on each side of the entrance and sealed them all in securely. We did all of this at night, you know, at midnight, in secret. Still today nobody outside the family except you knows this house has been cured. You I tell because you are like my daughter."

"Why, thank you, Doña Lucia," I replied, thrown off balance momentarily by the compliment. "That's the nicest thing anyone has said to me since I have been in San Juan."

"But Faustina didn't get well even after all this," continued Doña Lucia. "No, she got worse. Once she said a wind swept past her hammock in the night and something brushed against her arm. She had more trouble sleeping than before even and she was afraid to let me out of her sight. We were at wit's end, where could we turn?

"Then one day a messenger came from the temple in Santa Elena. You have heard about the señora who cures and her temple in Santa Elena, verdad?"

The temple Doña Lucia referred to was that of an *espirituista* or spiritualist, a person who has the power to divine the future and seek cures through contact with spirits of the dead. All of the several spiritualists I knew of were from other regions and kept their past to themselves.

"When she came here years ago she was a poor woman and now she is very rich, with helpers and a temple. She is famous as a diviner. The señora wished to see me because she had received a message for us, the messenger said. I don't know why I had not thought of consulting her myself. I went to see her.

"She said the spirit of Censo was restless because he had made a *promisa* (vow) to a saint that he had not been able to complete before his death. This was what was bothering Faustina—her father's spirit! The promise he had made was to make a pilgrimage to the Shrine of Esquipulas in Guatemala. I don't know why he made a promise or why he never told me about it. The señora said if Faustina would complete this promise of her father he would be content and his spirit would leave Faustina in peace.

"Some people do not believe in these things but the fact is that Faustina began to get better right away. Her appetite improved and she began to sleep and gain weight. It was only a few weeks until she felt well enough to go to Esquipulas. Magda and Sole took her, the three of them traveling by train. It was expensive, you bet, but a small price to pay for Faustina's health.

"Oh, no, I couldn't go! I had products coming in from the fields that I had to sell and I had to look after the animals. Ramon couldn't do all this alone.

"Faustina has never been sick since. Oh, that my son could have been cured so simply!

Faustina, though, was discovered to have a very serious case of diabetes a few months before my arrival in the field. Her illness after her father died may have been diabetes-connected too.

"So these are the things of our life here," Doña Lucia concluded wearily, shifting to a more comfortable position in the hammock. "But not all of life is sadness! Before many months we will be having the big wedding at Magda's."

10

Worst of Times

It was the month of the Fiesta of Santiago. Welcome rains had thrown a gossamer veil over the dust. The world became a great hothouse, with thick, tangled verdure reaching out twining, insistent fingers everywhere. The air, too pregnant to stir, hung heavy with moisture. Tiny unseen insects left pinpoints of blood on the ankles that endured for days and itched incessantly. With every scratch, a new and larger monument to the sancudo arose on the spot. Swarms of insects and heavy odors mark the rainy season as the fierce north wind of the other months becomes lethargic, then comatose—the air too heavy with humidity to stir.

Chica and I were at the far side of the pueblo, on our way home from one of our last interviews. As we sat down to rest and wait for the urbano on the stoop of a deserted building, Chica suddenly turned her face into her rebozo and jumped up, moving away with mouth covered.

"Oh, I can't bear the odor of pigs!" she cried.

We moved away down the steamy, fetid street, looking for a less aromatic spot in which to wait. I was surprised by her sudden outburst. The smell had not seemed unusually strong to me, but maybe I was becoming inured to the unpleasant odors which at first were so nauseous. The urbano soon lumbered around the corner, gears grinding, rooting its way through the muddy wallow that was the street. The incident of the pig odor slipped from my mind, its portent lost in the maze of anxieties and events that make up the fabric of anthropological fieldwork.

A day or so later when I stopped by Doña Lucia's I found Chica in tears and her mother angry. Cata was drinking again, I was told.

Doña Lucia was full of anger and resentment and glad to have an audience for all her grievances against him. He would drink for days, she said, as long as he could get credit at a cantina or borrow from friends. During these times he was unable to earn anything or care for his own land and animals. On this particular spree, he had neglected the team of oxen which Doña Lucia had contracted to him to such a degree that they were nearly dead from thirst when discovered in the field by a neighbor. Doña Lucia, rightfully furious, tore up the contract and reclaimed the oxen. Both legally and morally within her rights, she nonetheless placed Chica and Cata in an even more precarious economic situation by this action. Without the oxen Cata could only hire himself out at ten pesos a day, barely enough to pay for daily food for two persons, and that only on the days when there was work. With the oxen he could double his daily earnings and find work almost daily.

Chica was gray with anger at her mother. After all, she complained to me, was she not giving up everything to stay and care for her mother? And where was the thanks? I tried to calm Doña Lucia's anger, get her to reconsider, but she was too incensed. She wept and begged Chica to leave "that borracho," but vowed never to let him have another team of oxen of hers.

Privately Chica confided to me that she could not leave her husband. If she did, her children would have no father and she and they would be dependent upon the good will of her mother and brother. No, a woman who left her husband was worse off than dead, she was a slave, as Chica saw it. She had put up with Cata's drinking for nearly twenty years, it was not that bad. Besides, when he was sober Cata was a good husband and father.

Doña Lucia countered Chica's arguments with reminders, in my presence, of the many times Cata had beaten Chica, actually tried to kill her, when he was drunk. That, said Doña Lucia, was the undeniable and unforgivable fault from which Cata suffered. Doña Lucia continued to weep. Chica went about her tasks, waiting on her mother with dogged determination. After some time elapsed, she again begged her mother to let them use the oxen, but Doña Lucia would not relent.

The next day when I arrived at their house I found a grim-faced Chica busy making tortillas. This was something new. Most people purchased tortillas from the women in every neighborhood who made them for sale. I asked if she was going to be able to go out on an interview. No, she could not go this time because she had to make tortillas to sell in the plaza in order to earn money for her and Cata's supper, she said. She was never ever going to accept anything from her mother again.

Saying all this more for the benefit of Doña Lucia than me, she continued. She would care for her mother because it was her duty as a daughter but she would show her that she, Chica, was not dependent on others! I told her we could cancel the interview and I would help her, then we would go together to the plaza to sell the tortillas. My help was only by way of moral support, sympathy, and understanding, being altogether inept at tortilla making. As she patted out the tortillas one by one and placed them on the *comal* (clay griddle) to bake, we talked and she began to feel better.

By 1:00 p.m. the tortillas were ready, rather late to sell in the market for midday trade. The sun bore into our skulls and scorched the skin on our arms as we trudged through the muddy street to the plazita. Chica draped her rebozo over her head while I shaded myself as best I could with my portfolio. The streets were deserted. Even the mongrel dogs and the pigs had taken refuge in the knife blades of shade at the edge of buildings. We walked along in silence. I touched her hand and she turned to me with that sad smile I noticed so often these days.

"Listen," I said, "you don't need to sell tortillas. Let me pay you what I owe you for helping me as I did Betina when she was helping me." I had been keeping a record of the hours she helped me and intended to pay her one way or another before I left.

"No!" Her response was terse and determined and we both understood that selling the tortillas was a gesture of defiance and independence which she had to make in order to maintain her dignity and self-respect. If she sold them, she would earn barely enough to buy a meager supper for two people.

A week or so later Chica and I were driving the pick-up out to a *rancheria* to interview a male curer. Although curing was not the direct focus of the project, it seemed a good idea to interview this man whom I had heard was very successful as a curer and had an abiding interest in local history. We passed the green fields, the men plowing in their brightly colored homemade undershorts, plodding along behind their oxen-pulled plows. The mango and coconut trees swayed in the breeze. The fields and orchards were the prettiest part of the whole region and I enjoyed taking excursions into the countryside even though it meant negotiating the rutted, sometimes barely passable dirt roads.

"I liked it in the country. In the country we were content. Cata didn't drink and we had animals. In the country everything was nice and peaceful," Chica commented.

"Oh, when did you live in the country?" I asked, always interested in people's reminiscing about the past.

"When Anastasio was a baby. I think, no, I can't remember now how many years we lived in the milpa. At first we lived in San Juan with Cata's parents. That was where we went to live after the wedding. Did I ever tell you about our wedding? Oh, we had such a big wedding! It was a real traditional wedding in the church with all the old customs carried out beforehand. Cata's father and his relatives and compadres brought the young bull, the kid, the dozen hens, the bag of maize, all the traditional gifts, to my father's house the night before the wedding. Nobody does that anymore."

"We lived with Cata's parents for a few years after we married. But it was crowded and they were very poor. All those children and Cata one of the oldest. Then Cata got a job as a farm laborer. We moved out to the milpa. I remember that day! We found a little shady place at one end of the field where Cata was working and we sat there all day, I and Anastasio. Toward evening the señor came and said we could put up a little choza there if we wanted to. Later the other señor with land adjoining said, 'Oh, I see that you haven't much room here for your family. Go ahead and use a little bit of my field too. Raise your children here. Here is everything you need.'

"We put up the little reed choza and made the *enramada* (sunshade). We were very happy there. Relatives gave us a few turkey chicks and a goat. We planted a little garden. It wasn't long until we had animals to sell." She paused, lost in thought, then continued.

"But later Cata wanted to move back to San Juan. He said it was too dangerous in the milpa. Robbers might come at night and steal the animals. People are often murdered in the milpa, did you know? Oh, yes. Maybe robbers come to steal and somebody gets killed. Or someone has a grudge to bear so they come in the night to settle it while you are sleeping. So Cata wanted to move back to San Juan. Finally we had an opportunity to buy a house. The house was very small and it was not finished but it was cheap and in a good location close to the plazita, only a block from my sister's. We bought it, house and lot, for five thousand pesos. That was years ago and still my little house has no proper door."

"Who lives in your house now?"

"It's empty. No one wants to rent a house without a secure door that will lock."

"Maybe you should move back to your house," I suggested. "Couldn't Faustina and Magdalena take turns caring for your mother for a while?"

Chica did not think she could do this. As the eldest daughter, she felt it was her duty to care for their mother in the absence of a daughter-in-law in the house. Faustina had the baby to care for, she had diabetes and still was not strong after her operation. Magda had her hands full helping her husband with the store and cantina, plus three children.

I admired Chica's determination to care for Doña Lucia and I had some understanding of how difficult it was. Doña Lucia was losing strength and was becoming more and more of a burden. She had her good days and bad days, but the bad days were becoming more frequent, the good days fewer. On a bad day, she was incontinent, she coughed until she fell back exhausted in the hammock, she refused food, spat up blood, and wept at her own helplessness. At times in utter frustration at herself and her illness she reverted to infantile behavior, flinging her food to the floor and cursing Chica for some imagined mistake or failure. On such days there was no pleasing Doña Lucia. I sympathized with Chica, yet I could not be angry toward her mother. Doña Lucia was dying and she knew it.

When the Fiesta of Santiago arrived, Chica, who so dearly loved fiestas and dancing, was in full mourning for a recently deceased comadre. She would not be able to take part in the fiesta except to work in the preparation of food and help behind the scenes in other ways. Mourning women should not dance or appear to be enjoying themselves, but because Chica was helping me we could go to the afternoon dance as spectators. This we decided to do.

At the appointed hour Chica appeared in the street in front of Sole's cantina, freshly bathed, striking in sweeping black broken only by the turquoise satin ribbons she wore in her braids. We set off for the fiesta, she bemoaning the fact that she would not be able to dance. I was happy simply to be an observer.

In the street adjoining the central plaza we encountered the drunken Cata who recognized us in spite of his stupor and staggered toward us through the crowd of men drinking and talking around the beer kiosks. He called to Chica but she swept past, eyes straight ahead. Zapotec etiquette permits, even demands, that women ignore drunks, even if they happen to be one's husband or brother. Nonetheless, it was an embarrassing encounter for Chica. She did not enjoy the fiesta. After an hour or so, she suggested that we leave. Alberto, her twelve-year-old son, home on vacation for a few days, was leaving the next morning to return to the missionary school and she still had to launder his clothes.

The next day at noon as I returned home for lunch, I stopped at Sole's door.

"*Noo tu la*? Are you home?" I called into the silent cantina. Sole's voice echoed through the empty vaults of the vacant cantina, bidding me to enter. In the corredor of Sole's house at the back of the cantina I found Chica sitting on a little stool with her back to the door, her face buried in her rebozo. Sole, brows furrowed in their permanent frown, sat in the hammock facing her.

"*Ay, Dios mio*! What has happened?" I exclaimed. My mind raced ahead to possible disasters. Doña Lucia dead? An accident? I sat down in the other hammock and listened while Chica poured forth her latest woes amid renewed weeping and Sole's sympathetic cluckings.

Doña Lucia, being a provident woman, was preparing for the final social event of her life, her funeral. This morning she had commissioned her two other daughters, Faustina and Magda, to make a trip to Xochitlan to buy the black velvet and trimmings for her burial dress. Chica had not been told of the plans. As the eldest daughter she should have been entrusted with this traditional and sacred duty, she felt. She was crushed, inconsolable. They had purposely kept the plans secret from her, she sobbed. Her own family! Not even her own family respected her! They treated her no better than a common vallista who came to the house to do the laundry. As she bent into her rebozo, terrible sobs wracked her thin shoulders. Money talked, she wept. Because she was poor nobody respected her, not even her own family!

I had come to love and respect both Doña Lucia and Chica deeply in the many hours we had spent together. I was angry with Doña Lucia but still I could see her side of it. Chica's son, Alberto, was leaving this morning so she would not have been able to go today. Perhaps Magda and Faustina were going to Xochitlan for other business and she casually asked the two sisters to make the purchases while they were there. But I felt great empathy with Chica, too. She was so loving and generous with everyone, perhaps one of the reasons she could not hang on to a peso. I knelt on the floor with my arm around her shoulders and cradled her wet face against my chest.

"Never mind," I urged. "Just ignore it. Relatives are like that—insensitive and thoughtless even though they don't mean it." Then I found myself telling Chica and Soledad of wounds I had suffered in my own family when my father died years earlier, hurts so deep I had never before mentioned them to anyone.

When I finished, Chica dried her eyes on the corner of her rebozo and stared at her feet. "Yes, perhaps it's true. Perhaps all families have their troubles."

"Listen," I said, suddenly inspired. "I have to go to Oaxaca tomorrow to pick up some supplies and have some copying done. Come with me."

"Si, vamonos," she replied without enthusiasm while continuing to stare at her feet.

The next morning, halfway to Oaxaca Chica became nauseated. We stopped for half an hour beside the road. I had a couple of Dramamine tablets with me which I had thoughtlessly not offered her before we left. Belatedly I remembered that she had felt ill on our previous trip to Oaxaca. She took a tablet with a swallow of water, the nausea passed, and we continued on our way. She soon fell asleep. Glancing at her sleeping form, I noted for the first time that she had abandoned her mourning blacks temporarily for the more cheerful clothing appropriate for a holiday in the city.

The trip to Oaxaca was a relaxing time for both of us and a morale-booster for Chica. We rented a room at the hotel where I customarily stayed, the first time she had ever slept on a "gringa" bed. She refused to open her bed but slept on the bedspread, "so you won't have to pay extra," although I tried to explain that we were paying a small extra fee for two people whether or not she opened the bed. We sat at a sidewalk cafe with the "rich" American tourists and ordered drinks, I a margarita, she a beer. Street musicians were playing Isthmus music on their marimbas for the tourist trade. We requested "La Zandunga," "La Llorona," "Rancho Gubiña," (a favorite of mine) and "La Zandunga" again. We became a little giddy from the drinks and laughed more than we had in weeks.

During those few days we ate at the tourist dining rooms of "gringo" food she had never tasted, we shopped in the market for yardage and oilcloth which Doña Lucia had commissioned us to buy, probably to make amends for her oversight about the funeral apparel. Chica bargained for two days off and on for some mango baskets, and we visited the cathedral and museum of archaeological treasures.

Chica's spirits were up. We laughed and chattered as we walked the streets while tourists and townspeople alike stared after us. Mestizos threw us disapproving glances at what they considered inappropriate behavior, a gringa and a tehuana arm-in-arm. The tourists, unaware of Mexican social class barriers, simply looked at us with mild curiosity, smilingly inquiring where Chica, in her flowing skirts and burgundy huipil, was from. Chica carried off her role of visiting tourist perfectly, feigning complete self-confidence as if she lived everyday of her life thus. She had an abundance of that sometimes admirable human quality, pride, and this, coupled with keen intelligence, sensitivity, and flexibility, gave her a facade of queenly elegance.

I bought a couple of U.S. fashion magazines from a store which dealt in such exotica and we amused ourselves during siesta hours lying on our beds thumbing through the books. She could not read a word of Spanish, much less English, but she adored the fashion books and studied them assiduously. The miniskirt and dark, thick stockings were just appearing on the U.S. fashion scene. I made unflattering criticisms of the new fashions, declaring I would never be caught alive or dead in those ridiculous garments. Chica stared and stared at the grotesquely made-up models in their preposterous poses. I expected her to be shocked, for it was then quite improper for a San Juan woman even to show her ankles in public. I asked what she thought of the clothes.

"Oh, I don't know," she commented at length. "After all, the legs are covered, and if everybody is wearing them . . ."

Here, I thought, was a natural anthropologist, willing to accept other people's customs and behavior and try to understand them in what she imagined to be their own cultural context. I knew so many adults in my own country who never seemed able to grasp what Chica did not have to be taught, cultural relativity.

Home again in San Juan the pleasures of the city soon evaporated into dim, chimeric memories. We still had to complete at least a couple of the questionnaires and my time for fieldwork was running short. I would be leaving for home in a few weeks. We spent two or three days working hard. Chica had become tired and sad again. I thought it best to drive the pick-up on our rounds even though walking was far easier for me than maneuvering the truck in and out of Tiu Tono's narrow entrance.

As we drove along through the mud-choked streets, I related news gathered earlier in El Centro. The lawyer son of Doña Maria, who lived in Mexico City, had brought his wife and children for a visit and they had taken a San Juan girl home to the city with them as a servant.

"Verdad?" she commented. "How much are they paying her?"

"I heard two hundred pesos per month plus room and board."

Chica was silent for a time and then said, half to herself, "Yes, if I were young again that is what I would do. Instead of marrying at age fifteen I would go to Mexico (City) and find a job as a servant girl."

Again silence reigned. We bumped along the street, the shock-absorbers of the pick-up long since worn out.

"I almost went to Mexico City once," she continued. "It was when my Tio Carlos came to take Ramon to Mexico City to go to school. Ramon was only five or so and I was maybe twelve. My uncle said one of the girls should go along so that Ramon did not become homesick. I had my clothes all washed, ironed, and packed in my basket. But when my tio came for us, he stared and stared at me and then he said to my mother, 'It's better that Sefa goes. She is nearer Ramon's age. Chica is too pretty and she will soon marry.' Oh, how I hated my uncle at that moment!" She began to cry, remembering.

I did my best to think of something cheerful but could not. We were passing the cemetery.

I asked myself why Chica would stay with Cata, with his drinking and violence. Chica's explanations did not seem an adequate reason to continue such an existence. I thought the drinking and Chica's poor health were the reasons for their poverty and, according to Doña Lucia, Cata was insanely jealous even when sober. Why, lamented Doña Lucia, her daughter could not even bathe and put on fresh clothing without being accused of having a lover waiting for her somewhere. Every man in San Juan was suspect except family. When Cata was drunk he became violent and once even tried to kill Chica, Doña Lucia had confided. Knowing the quiet, gentle Cata sober, it was difficult to believe that he could change so drastically under the influence of alcohol.

We had a difficult time making our last interview. Several times in as many days, Chica begged off at the last minute, promising to go "*mañana*." This was not her usual cooperative response and I wondered if I had somehow offended her. Toward the end of the week, though, she was ready when I came for her. We finished the interview and sat on a rock beside the street to wait for the urbano.

"Next summer when I come back—," I began. We had been planning for some time all the things we would do "next summer when I return." I would not be burdened with project work and we could truly relax and enjoy ourselves, go places, and do things together simply for the fun of it. I thought Chica might like to visit the pilgrimage sites of Esquipulas in Guatemala and Astata, closer to San Juan, neither of which I had seen. She interrupted me in mid-sentence.

"I won't be here next summer when you come back."

In her usual sad, matter-of-fact way, she continued, "No, I won't be here next year. I'll be in the cemetery."

"*What*? What did you say?" I thought I must have misunderstood or that she was making a bad joke. I was trying to catch her eye but she avoided looking at me. Yes, she sighed, she was going to die because she was pregnant. The doctor had told her last time that she could not endure another difficult labor.

"But you *said* you could not get pregnant!" I heard myself shrieking, inexplicably angry as one is at first overcome with anger when a loved one suddenly dies. She began to cry. I leaned over and put my arm around her shoulder and we just sat there for a few minutes.

"Well, maybe it's not true that you are pregnant," I said, knowing that it was. The incidents of nausea, the car sickness, the fatigue of the past few weeks, all pointed in the same direction.

I stood up. She remained hunched over, head bent, her old black rebozo draped over her head and falling across the side of her face. She looked like a sad madonna, a 17th-century artist's portrayal of the holy mother. Rising, she wiped her eyes with the corner of the rebozo, imploring me not to tell anyone, especially not her mother.

We walked along the street toward home in silence, the bus forgotten, time and the world forgotten. I was too stunned to make any constructive suggestions. I knew her health was poor, I was by now sure she had diabetes which was not being treated, and she had already endured ten full-term pregnancies in just over twenty years of marriage. I knew enough about health, diabetes, and pregnancy to know it was entirely possible that she could not survive another birth.

That night, sleepless in my hammock, I had time to consider the problem more rationally. What should we do? What were the possibilities? At length I decided that we should go to the local doctor first and get his opinion. Perhaps the situation was not as serious as Chica thought. Maybe she had misunderstood the doctor two years ago after her last stillbirth. With good prenatal care, perhaps she had a very substantial chance of bringing forth a live, healthy baby. I could help pay her medical expenses which, by U.S. standards, would be modest. In the small hours of the morning I fell asleep with a plan to take her to the doctor the following day.

It was a week before I was able to get her to go with me to the doctor. When we were finally in his office, the bad news confirmed, she surprised me by asking the doctor how she could get an abortion. Dr. Mario explained to her in Zapotec and to me in Spanish that he was sorry but he could not perform an abortion because it was an illegal procedure. He could, however, care for her after an abortion performed illegally by someone else but he strongly advised against it as highly dangerous for her because he had confirmed her suspicion of diabetes. He treated Doña Lucia frequently for diabetes and was well acquainted with the family's health problems. Worse, he said, Chica seemed to be already four or five months into the pregnancy. He wrote a note for the pharmacist prescribing multiple vitamins she should take and advised a series of injections to "build her up" in view of the diabetes. The birthdate, he thought, would be late January. I would be gone by then so I arranged with the doctor to prepay some of her future medical expenses.

Dr. Mario was a native son of the pueblo, one of those rare individuals who make a great personal sacrifice to serve their people after having once escaped from the misery and poverty of the place. I thought he earned too little respect for his sacrifice. Indeed, the people did not even realize what a sacrifice it was to practice medicine here rather than in a large city with modern hospitals. Some people were jealous because he drove a Volkswagen bug and could afford to invest in land and property on occasion. He was the only Zapotec doctor in the area and the only doctor in San Juan, yet many people preferred to visit doctors in El Centro or in Xochitlan or even Mexico City when they had the money.

On the way home from the doctor's office, Chica again mentioned her intention of seeking an abortion. There was a woman in Xochitlan who performed them. What did I think? I was opposed to the idea for the reasons Dr. Mario had mentioned. I explained that I would be in favor if she could have an abortion in a modern hospital, if her health was better, and if the pregnancy was not so far advanced. Privately, I thought it rather unlikely that she could survive an abortion under the best of circumstances, and an illegal abortion was certainly not that. The next morning I went early to El Centro purposely to buy the vitamins the doctor had ordered.

Over the next few days, Chica was very depressed. She had nobody but me to share her bad news with at the moment and I was sworn to silence. A week passed and she had not taken any of the vitamins. Worse, she still wanted the abortion. Why should she take vitamins, she said glumly, they just made larger babies (a local rumor). I was edgy because I expected her to ask me to take her to find the abortionist in Xochitlan. If discovered, we could be jailed, especially me, the collaborating foreigner. The possible consequences for her undergoing an illegal and probably unprofessional abortion were too chilling even to consider. But if she asked, I knew I would not refuse.

As the days passed, she quit mentioning the possibility of abortion and finally even visited the doctor for the first of the series of injections. Although she still had not told her mother, she shared the news with Cata who seemed to take a firm hold on himself, began working every day, and determinedly avoided the cantinas. Chica's energy was very low, causing her to sleep during siestas, something she normally never did, and I suspected that Doña Lucia had already guessed her secret.

11

Misfortune, Good Fortune

I had come to love my House-on-the-Hill with its rooftop vistas and the spacious, cool veranda which faced east into the morning sun. My early efforts at keeping curtains on the windows proved much too daunting a task. After I had persisted in picking them up out of the corners the wind had flung them into night after night for weeks, I did what a more sensible person might have done from the first—folded them and put them away. For privacy, I painted the glass in the bedroom windows to make it opaque. True, there were still no barriers on the windows, not even insect screens, but I had become quite accustomed to the situation.

When I first moved in it was cool November and I slept with the windows locked shut, leaving the transoms open for air. Over the months however, the nights became warmer and I had been sleeping with the windows wide open for weeks.

The six-month lease still had about a month to run and I had not given it much thought, assuming that we would renew it for the last three months of my stay. Then one morning on my way out, Tiu Tono stopped me.

"Are you moving when your lease is up?" he asked.

"No, I did not plan to. I will still be here three months after our present lease expires. I thought perhaps we could renew the lease," I suggested innocently.

"Ah, yes, we can do that, señorita. However, I have to raise the rent. I am an old man and have many medical expenses, you know," he said, by way of preparing me for the bad news.

"What rent were you thinking of?" I asked.

He named a figure *three times* more than I had been paying. I was speechless. True, I had been paying low rent but I had also invested a good sum in making the house liveable; improvements that would still be in the house after I left. I had justified the costly improvements mainly because the rent was low.

"Well, I am sorry, Tiu Tono, but that is just more than I can afford to pay. I will have to look for another place."

I left in a fury. The last thing I needed was to spend time looking for another place to live, moving, and getting settled again in these last months of fieldwork when there where so many tasks still to complete.

I asked my friends and compadres what I should do. They promised to help me find another place. I consulted a lawyer in El Centro who said I would have to move if we could not agree on some intermediate figure. Houses were hard to find in San Juan. The several houses that might be available were unimproved, without electricity or water and with dirt floors. I had almost decided I would have to pay Tiu Tono's exorbitant price when Doña Lucia and Chica suggested that I move to Doña Lucia's house. Chica had already asked her brother, Ramon, about it and he had agreed to have two rooms fixed up for me by putting in windows and adding a cement floor to the one without a floor. He said he had planned to make those improvements anyway and might as well do it now.

I dropped the news of my prospective new home into the ear of Rufina, Tiu's daughter. Faced with the prospect of losing his tenant altogether, Tiu Tono was more amenable to negotiating. After a couple of weeks of sparring, we agreed that I would pay double the previous rent for the last three months of my stay. Although agreeing to Tiu's demands was a bitter pill to swallow, I thought the time saved by not moving was more important than my pride.

Since first moving in I had experienced a few problems with petty vandalism. Nothing serious, but twice the button to my electric doorbell was torn out of the wall beside the gate. I then rigged up a bell on my veranda attached to a long rope, the end of which hung outside the gate. If naughty little boys cut off the rope, it was easy and cheap to replace.

Little boys had also been breaking the window panes with slingshots, usually when I was away from the house. The windows, the kind with many small panes, made irresistible targets from the path along the river. It seemed futile to replace every little broken pane, in Mexico the renter's responsibility. As the months passed, some rear windows had nearly every pane missing.

Then one night not long after we had renegotiated the lease, I was awakened by glass showering over me and the bed. Still half asleep, I stumbled to the window shouting obscenities in Zapotec and Spanish, an automatic reaction I had long since learned from San Juan women. The street below was pitch black. What had happened to the dim street lamp around the curve? I moved out of the bedroom into the hammock on the veranda and went back to sleep, telling myself the stone throwers were just mischievous youngsters trying to scare the gringa. The next morning I was alarmed to find a rock bigger than a baseball in the corner of the bedroom. I showed the rock to Rufina and we agreed that it was probably just naughty little boys.

The following night I was again startled by a barrage of rocks pounding the house. This time I was frightened even though the rocks failed to find their marks and no windows were broken. Again I could see no one in the street below. It was early, about 10:00 p.m., and I had not retired for the night. I decided to close the bedroom windows and sleep again on the veranda. Hammock sleeping was never comfortable for me, so the next night, weary from two nights in the hammock, I retired early to the bedroom.

At midnight I awakened with a start to footsteps crunching the dry brush outside my windows. In the dim light I could make out the silhouettes of two men. When I screamed, they ducked out of sight. Terrified, I ran down the hill to Tiu's door where I pounded and yelled for what seemed like an hour. At last Rufina opened the door. I was near hysteria but she calmed me enough to learn what had occurred. She lit a lantern and we went out into the street together. The lamp over Tiu's entrance had been destroyed by a well-aimed rock, leaving the street as black as a woman's mourning skirts. Not a sound came from the street. After a few minutes of thinking about what I should do, I asked Rufina to accompany me to my house to get my hammock. I would go to Doña Lucia's for the remainder of the night.

I settled into the hammock at Doña Lucia's but remained wide-eyed and sleepless. About two hours later, around 3:00 a.m., when everyone else was deep in sleep, two or three people ran through the alley past Doña Lucia's house, banging on the metal gate as they passed. The would-be intruders had been watching and knew that I went to this house to sleep. Everyone was instantly awake and several of us went out into the street with lights, armed with clubs and rocks, to give chase. The men followed the culprits down to the river where they lost the trail.

To this day, I prefer to think it was just a Saturday night prank for some idle youths from across the river. I had been living in the house alone too long and the word had spread. Without bars on the windows, the little *gringuita* alone in the house was too tempting and easy a target to pass up. The rock throwing was probably a preliminary test to see what I would do, to see if I was alone and whether I had a gun to protect me.

For several nights I took my hammock down to Doña Lucia's at dusk. Although thieves could enter the house, there was not much there worth stealing—folding and rough-hewn furniture, my old portable typewriter, books and office supplies. As far as we could determine, nobody entered although we found footprints in the loose dust outside the bedroom windows.

Knowing I could not sleep well in the hammock, after a few nights Chica insisted that she and Cata sleep at my house so I could rest properly in my own bed. I consented but only until I could find a velador to sleep on the veranda regularly. The two of them came up each night after dusk and slept in the hammocks on the veranda while I occupied the adjacent bedroom. Chica was urging me to move into Doña Lucia's house. Ramon still wanted to fix up the rooms for me. If I came to live there, Chica and Cata could go back to their own house, at least at night. They insisted I should pay no rent for the remaining few months of my project. Doña Lucia, having guessed Chica's condition, was making less demands on her and had hired a twelve-year-old neighbor child to help around the house and run errands. I decided to move to Doña Lucia's.

While the work was being done on the rooms I continued to stay in the House-on-the-Hill, finally able to persuade a fourteen-year-old neighbor boy to sleep every night on the veranda. Chica insisted I take Cata's pistol and keep it loaded and within easy reach. I was instructed to fire it into the air anytime something suspicious occurred. A few days later, when someone pulled the doorbell rope late at night I discharged the weapon skyward as instructed. The pistol and the fourteen-year-old velador assuaged my fears reasonably well for a few days. Then the velador announced that he would not stay nights unless he could sleep inside my office-parlor with the door locked. I was paying him to sleep on the veranda and was firm about it. He stopped coming.

Project work had been piling up due to my preoccupation with the intruders and the problems of staying in the house but preparing to move. Once again I was sleeping fitfully at Doña Lucia's each night. Installing the windows and laying the concrete floor were taking longer than anyone imagined but things were moving slowly ahead.

It was now within weeks of the end of my fieldwork. I began to tie up the loose ends of information and to make the rounds of the dozens of people who had helped me, to thank them and bid them goodbye. One of the first places I went was to the school to thank the headmaster for giving me data on school attendance, curricula, and such. The headmaster had changed since the school census was taken when I first moved to San Juan. While we were talking, I noticed on his desk a folder marked in bold letters *Censo*.

"Is that by any chance the school census?" I inquired, trying to act casual.

"Yes, would you like to see it?"

Trying to control my excitement, I answered yes as casually as possible. Mentally I was thinking: What a stroke of luck! At last, the school census I had chased so fruitlessly months earlier was right here in my hands—the census with the name, age, and sex of every member of every household in San Juan. It would be invaluable not only to my present project but in future fieldwork as well. Through the census one could locate people in the years to come to determine who was still in the pueblo five or ten years hence, to serve as a basis for tracing others, whether relocated or deceased, and to calculate the number of people moving into and out of the pueblo and what natural population increase had occurred.

It was a Friday afternoon and the schoolmaster said I could review the file over the weekend but he had to have it back by the opening of the school day Monday. Calmly thanking him while my heart pounded furiously, I took the census folder and went home. Now what was I to do? The nearest copy machine was in Oaxaca, four hours away over mountain roads and even if I went, the business would be closed for the weekend. But if I let this document slip through my hands I would never have another chance to get the 1967 census. I decided to try typing a copy and do as much as I could by Monday morning, which would be better than doing nothing. The census was hand-written but legible. I began to type immediately. It went faster than I imagined. For once, I was thankful for the years I had spent as a stenographer. There were only seven columns: the household number, name, age, sex, whether literate or not, occupation, and street address. I decided to chance staying in the House-on-the Hill alone with only the borrowed pistol for security over the weekend rather than go down to Doña Lucia's house at dusk, before they retired for the night. By Monday morning I had copied the whole census, seventy single-spaced pages of columns.

Now I needed more time in San Juan to contact some of the people listed in the census and to ask informants about relationships between households. I also needed to make a spot-check of the accuracy of the names, ages, and occupations and to check it against the nearly two hundred families Doña Lucia had recalled from memory. I wrote to my doctoral committee at the university asking for a three-month extension of the field period, mentioning the important fact that I did not need any additional research funds.

When I returned the census, the schoolmaster asked if I had seen the census for the other school at the far end of the pueblo. Oh, no! I had not even thought about the other school. He told me to ask the schoolmaster there and sent a note along with me requesting that he allow me to review it. In a couple of days I had another long census, that when typed, totalled fifty-four pages. The important thing was that I had a *complete census of San Juan* for the year 1967. That census is still in my files and it has proven its worth several times during subsequent fieldwork.

Now that I was staying longer, I began to arrange my belongings in readiness for the move to Doña Lucia's. I packed things I would not need again so they could be left in the pick-up undisturbed until I was ready to leave the field. When the windows were installed, they considerably brightened my sadness at having to leave the House-on-the-Hill. Facing southwest, the windows commanded a matchless view of the mountains and the spectacular sunsets which characterize the Isthmus. All that remained to be done before I could move in was the cement floor. Days passed and still the cement workers did not come despite repeated prodding by Doña Lucia's messengers. The morning after I completed copying the census, Tiu Tono called out to me as I hurried past his door.

"Oh, señorita, have you heard? There was a fight last night at Lucia's. Ramon beat up Cata and threw him into the street. I hear Cata has broken bones." Tiu Tono seemed pleased to pass along this unpleasant news.

I hurried down to Doña Lucia's. Yes, it was true, said Doña Lucia. Cata had come home drunk and begun an argument with Chica which ended in his trying to strangle her. Ramon came home about that time, and furious at Cata's actions, landed a few well-aimed punches before throwing Cata into the street, telling him never to step inside the house again. Cata had not suffered any broken bones after all and was already walking around the pueblo, still stone drunk.

The next day I had to drive to Oaxaca to attend a meeting with all the other anthropologists working in the Valley of Oaxaca. This was the only occasion during the entire year that presented an opportunity to compare the data I was collecting with that of several others similarly occupied in the very different villages of the Valley of Oaxaca. I returned to find the workers laying the concrete floor.

Doña Lucia was pleased that I was going to be living under her roof for a few weeks. I asked when I should make arrangements to move my belongings.

"Yes, I have been thinking about that too," she said. "I think what you should do is move one piece after dark each night so the neighbors won't know what you are doing."

I countered that I thought this might take too much time, maybe several weeks. I would never be moved in. Doña Lucia had never been up the hill to my house and did not know the nature of my possessions. I explained to her that my belongings were nothing special, just a couple of folding lawn chairs and an old card table plus some shelves and work tables of rough lumber. A portable typewriter, my bed, and a bare minimum of pots and dishes were the only other major articles. The rest were just boxes of books, notes, and office supplies. We discussed the move off and on for a couple of days. She was afraid if the neighbors saw all of these things coming in to her house at one time, someone would be envious and place a curse on her family.

"I have always done all my business at night and I have never had any trouble with my neighbors. Why, even during all the years I was buying corn to sell I never had it delivered during daylight hours. Someone would surely become jealous. My caution has avoided much trouble. Take my advice," she counseled.

"But these are my possessions so why would someone be envious of you, Doña Lucia?"

"Just take my advice and avoid trouble for us all."

I brought a few boxes down one per evening as she suggested. When I told her how many days I calculated it would take me to move at that rate she relented and consented to let me move my things over the course of two or three nights. Ramon and a hired neighbor were to do the moving.

The night before I was scheduled to move, Tiu Tono died in his sleep. Now I knew the moving would have to be postponed at least until after the eight-day initial mourning period. As a "daughter of the house" in the eyes of the community I would have to observe the death rituals and refrain from openly working during those days too. If I did otherwise it would alienate me from many people and create a scandal. How could I be so brash and uncaring after living (even as a renter) on his property for months? Besides, Doña Lucia warned me that I had better be especially careful in observing all the respectful obligations toward the departed Tiu because of my past conflict with him. If I did not, she said, his spirit could haunt me for the rest of my days and cause me unimaginable trouble, possibly even death.

The day Tiu died, his neighbors offered their services to Rufina even though many had barely been on speaking terms with Tiu Tono because of his stinginess, truculence, and outspoken disbelief in the power and sacredness of the saints. Ramon and two other neighbors prepared the body for burial by binding the lower limbs together and the arms to the torso so that it would lie flat, and then dressing the body in the burial clothes—a white shirt and black trousers.

These preparations complete, the corpse was laid to rest on a bed of clean river sand in front of the household shrine where it would remain, surrounded by flowers and frequently incensed with copal, until shortly before the funeral. Four beeswax candles about three feet tall and five inches in diameter were put in place and lighted, two at the head and two at the feet of the body. A white handkerchief covered the face.

Neighborhood women and his few female relatives gathered in the small, dark room lit only by the four candles and began their praying, chanting, and ritual weeping, led by a hired woman *rezadora* (prayer leader). The women, usually six to a dozen at any one time, knelt on woven mats facing the altar, their black rebozos drawn over their heads, and their bare feet protruding from the rear folds of their long, black skirts. The shutters were tightly closed, and the little room was stifling with so many people, the air heavy with incense. Each prayer set, a *rosario*, lasted between fifteen and twenty minutes. Then, except for close female relatives (in this case, the daughter Rufina), the women would file out, pressing their contributions of three pesos each into Rufina's hand. Other women filed in to take their places as another rosario began. The rosarios would continue throughout the day and night until the church mass and burial.

Men came to pay their respects and their contributions of five pesos but they were not required to take part in the prayers said in the room

Women's contingent, funeral procession

where the body lay. Instead they sat in the corredor and toasted each contributing male mourner in turn with a shot of mezcal, much as they did at the fiestas. An elderly man acted as the official incenser who, at intervals, brought a small incense burner into the room where the body lay, carefully offered incense to the four directions indicated by the four candles and to the altar, all the while chanting prayers.

The rosarios were always an ordeal for me. I could not endure the thick rebozo drawn around the head, the lack of air, and the dense, heavy scent of burning copal. At the previous rosarios in which I had participated, it took every trick of imagination to fight back the threatening nausea. This time, I attended the first rosario before the heat became unbearable and spent the rest of the day in the House-on-the-Hill, privately catching up on the pile of field notes always awaiting attention. If Tiu Tono's spirit noticed my breach of funerary etiquette, there was no indication of it.

Burials usually take place on the same day that the death occurs in this hot climate, devoid of an embalming process. Tiu's mass and burial, though, had to be postponed more than twenty-four hours to allow time for his son to arrive from Mexico City. The rosarios continued throughout the night.

In the morning, the men who would act as pallbearers placed Tiu in his coffin—the usual roughhewn wood box—and carried it to the church for the mass. Considering his stand on the saints and the church, I wondered if he was protesting this travesty of his principles from another world. When the mass ended, the long procession to the cemetery began. The distance was more than a mile, the morning was hot, and even though the women were always the last group in the funeral procession and thus farthest from the coffin at its head, I had to catch my breath several times as the nauseating, sick smell of death swept over the mourners. The coffin-bearers, wearing handkerchiefs tied over their noses and mouths, staggered under their heavy burden and the stench, stopping every hundred meters or so to change shifts.

The old man buried at last, the people straggled away from the cemetery in knots of two and three. I too began the long trek home, lagging behind to observe the mourners. There were not many, it was the smallest funeral I had witnessed here. Nobody I knew well except Ramon, Rufina, and a couple of other neighbors were in sight. Neither

Chica nor Doña Lucia attended because death rituals and funerals are considered dangerous for pregnant women and persons in poor health. An elderly lady, a distant relative of Doña Lucia, joined me and began to talk.

"My, what a small funeral! Not even his own brother and family came! That is what happens when one cannot get along with one's neighbors and kin. It is such a pity to have to travel to the cemetery almost alone, though. That should be a lesson to other people who think they can live without the help of their family and neighbors!"

We returned to Tiu's house and were served the hot meal demanded by custom, though no one had much appetite. The sand on which Tiu Tono had lain in front of the altar was now heaped with flowers, giving the appearance of a fresh grave mound. Around this mound there would be rosarios every evening for the next eight days and Rufina would be expected to spend most of those eight days praying and weeping before it, accompanied by her two elderly aunts. I would have to attend a rosario every night too, but only one, and of course I would pay my contribution to each. At the end of the *novena* all the flowers, whether dead or fresh, all the sand, the candles, and the two bricks on which the head of the corpse had rested would be gathered up and taken to the cemetery to be carefully placed on the new grave.

Having been in close contact with the corpse during the preceding days, I, like all the other mourners, was now contaminated with the "heat of the dead"—an essence which is not especially harmful to healthy persons but is highly dangerous for persons in poor health, pregnant women, babies and toddlers. Since the "heat" is transmittable, it would be unthinkable for me to visit Doña Lucia or Chica or any other household where there might be susceptible people until I had bathed, washed my hair, and laundered all the clothing I had been wearing since the death.

Women were always concerned about my hair after funerals because I wore it short and curled, and they could not tell by looking at it whether or not it was freshly shampooed. The very thick hair of San Juan women stayed damp for hours after being washed and was worn loose to let it air dry, making it easy to determine freshly washed locks. In order to put everyone's mind at ease, I waited two days before visiting Doña Lucia and then went with my hair still in rollers so there would be no question about my having taken the proper precautions.

The first thing Doña Lucia asked me was if I had noticed any strange movements of air or noises in my house or around the pick-up which had been parked just a few feet from where Tiu died. I had not.

"Well, just be very, very careful until after the novena," she warned. "Don't do anything which might cause Tono's spirit to be angry!" I promised to watch my step. That night when I returned to Tiu Tono's at dusk, I gave the pick-up, still parked a few feet from where Tiu Tono died, an extra-wide berth. How perfectly ridiculous, I scolded myself. Turning, I resolutely went back, unlocked the covered canopy, and peered in. Nothing but emptiness. Better get hold of yourself, I thought, you are beginning to believe in spirits! Yes, it was just as well that I would soon be going home.

The closing months of fieldwork are always the busiest and the most rewarding. At last, one knows enough about the culture to begin getting new insights and recognizing new patterns of behavior daily, and because of this, new questions present themselves continually. Field data come at a furious pace and in mostly informal encounters. I wrote up notes for an hour or two whenever the opportunity arose, day or night. In a way I was thankful for the time Tiu Tono's death rituals allowed me for catching up and organizing the remainder of the fieldwork.

12

Shattered Windows, Shattered Lives

As soon as the mourning period for Tiu Tono was over, Doña Lucia again arranged a night when Ramon and the helper could begin moving me. Then, before moving night arrived, there was more trouble in Doña Lucia's home. Cata, forbidden to enter the house, threw rocks and broke out almost all the new window panes, either in revenge against Doña Lucia and Ramon or to vent his resentment toward Chica, who had again stayed overnight with her mother. Whatever his reason, he had taken out his anger on the new window panes.

The news was broken to me by Sole as I took the shortcut through her cantina next morning. Everyone thought it was good luck that Ramon was not home when the windows were broken. Chica was weeping when I arrived and Doña Lucia was scolding.

"Whatever is the matter with my daughter? Is she *loca* (crazy)? Why would a woman stay with a drunken bum and suffer for years and years? I have begged her time and time again, 'Leave that man. He will kill you if you stay with him.' I have tried to help her, her sisters and her brother have tried to help and protect her but she will not protect herself! Now somebody will probably get killed when Ramon comes back." Doña Lucia, weak and distraught, sobbed into her rebozo.

"Doesn't Ramon know yet?" I asked.

"No, he came home very late last night and went right to sleep. The door to that room was closed so he did not see the windows when he left for work early this morning. When he comes home today who knows what will happen!"

Comadre Jonsa, 1967

Compadre and author, 1990

The new market, 1975

Preparing to harvest mangoes

Friends, 1990

Women paying fiesta contributions (Credit Marsha Lieberman)

Women's wedding group

Trading in San Marcos

Going to clean graves, Todos Santos week

Street scene, 1975

Day's end, 1982

Mounted contingent, fiesta parade

Farewell dinner for Sandy, 1982

Doña Lucia was still crying while Chica, now dry-eyed, grimly served coffee and sweet bread to her mother sitting in the hammock. I opened the door and looked into the room that was to be my new home. Shattered glass was everywhere.

"But where are the rocks?" I asked, realizing that it would take a good many rocks to break that many panes. Chica said she had taken them out early in the morning. But when I looked out the broken windows I noticed that there were a number of good-sized rocks strewn about the corral that had not been there before. It appeared to me that the rocks had been thrown *out* as well as *in* the windows. It did not take much imagination to picture an angry Chica pitching the rocks back at Cata and possibly breaking more windowpanes in the process, but this was merely a suspicion. I said nothing.

"The only way is to get the windows repaired before Ramon comes home tonight, that's the only way to avoid trouble. If we hurry, maybe he won't even know they were broken," said Doña Lucia, dipping a piece of the roll into her coffee with trembling hand.

She had already sent the twelve-year-old servant girl to tell Magda to come and to contact Faustina. The parents and brother and sisters of Cata were also notified of the trouble. When Magda arrived a few minutes after I did, Doña Lucia sent her to the office of the presidente to file a formal complaint against Cata. This resulted in Cata being jailed within the hour. Faustina arrived by taxi a short time later, carrying the nursing Terecita.

The presidente informed Cata that he would stay in jail until the windows were repaired, but he told Magda that he could not keep Cata in jail more than a day or two.

Doña Lucia sent for the repairman to come and tell her how much the repairs would cost, and to begin work on replacing the panes. Within a couple of hours Cata's two youngest sisters, unmarried and about twenty years old, arrived with 150 pesos raised among Cata's family which they gave Doña Lucia as a down-payment, promising to return later with the remaining balance of fifty pesos. Doña Lucia had calmed down now that it appeared her plan would work.

Then at noon Ramon returned home unexpectedly. He very rarely came home at midday because he was usually miles away, collecting weekly payments on contracts of people who had purchased trucks and automobiles from the agency where he worked. Nobody breathed as he walked directly to the room and opened the door. Outwardly he remained calm and without uttering a word he turned on his heel and left the house. He had probably already received news of the broken windows by grapevine. In any case, he did not return home for two days and nights. When he did return, the windows were repaired, Cata was out of jail, Chica and Cata had gone back to their own house, and as far as I know the affair was never mentioned again by anyone.

This incident reinforced my growing conviction that women were a major force in peace-keeping, conflict avoidance, and conflict resolution in the pueblo. By now I had observed at least a dozen instances, most of them less dramatic than the window case, in which San Juan women, both relatives and neighbors, cooperated to avert confrontations between men. I also knew by now that there was a high incidence of homicide in the pueblo, having recorded seven during the first eleven months of fieldwork. I did not know if this was a regular pattern then but over the years of fieldwork since, I have found seven homicides per year about average for San Juan, a rate we in the United States would consider alarmingly high in a community of under eight thousand people. All the homicides known to me during the past twenty-five years I have worked in San Juan have been men and usually men under forty years of age. Women are well aware of the consequence for the entire family of a violent confrontation between men. Even if neither is killed, at least one will probably have to leave the pueblo for years, even permanently, in order to survive, and there remains the threat that one of the people involved might take revenge on any member of the other's family or their property.

* * *

Ramon's house, as Doña Lucia always referred to her home, was one of the largest in San Juan. Unlike the typical house of one room and corredor, Ramon's house boasted one very large room, the two smaller rooms which I would be occupying, a bathroom, and a roofed granary, all connected by a roofed breezeway and built around an ample courtyard. Like Topsy,* the house had just grown, whenever Ramon

* A character in Harriet Beecher Stowe's *Uncle Tom's Cabin*.

had a little extra money to make improvements. The kitchen was outside the house in the traditional way, far removed from the living area, and with only a sunshade, making it unusable in rainy weather. When it rained Doña Lucia used the breezeway between the house and granary for cooking because it had a tile roof which kept the dirt passageway dry. Even when it was not raining, Doña Lucia preferred to do her cooking here now when she was able to cook. Perching the round-bottomed pot over a hearth made of three stones, she fed a small stick of firewood into the coals gradually to keep the fire evenly hot while conserving fuel. When I moved in I set up a two-burner kerosene stove in my room but Doña Lucia did not like it. She said it made the whole place smell like petroleum. I seldom used it, cooking instead over the three-stone hearth in the breezeway when I needed to cook something.

Furnishings in San Juan houses are few and simple. Ramon's house was not exceptional in this respect. A long, rough dining table covered with oilcloth and flanked by two long benches sat in the breezeway. One end of the table was kept more or less clear so that one or two persons could take a meal there, but for the most part the table served as a storage area.

Among the pots, pans, spoons, and bowls stored on the table, one was apt to find a clove of garlic, a few dried shrimp and some bits of crumbled cheese in a saucer, leftover tortillas rapidly becoming chicken feed as they dried stiff, a small paper bag of salt (in rainy season always soaking wet), half a lemon, two or three dried chiles, a few dirty cups and spoons, and maybe a small half-green, half-rotten tomato. This was the extent of most houses' larder. Having no way to preserve food, almost nothing was kept on hand.

Eating arrangements are very informal in San Juan. Except on ritual occasions, meals are casual affairs, with perhaps two people eating at the same time, more by accident than by plan. The woman of the house helps herself from whatever is in the pot on the stove when she is hungry and has the time, and serves the adult males of the household when they seat themselves at the table. Children over eight help themselves. Not infrequently, no cooking has been done for the day because of other more urgent tasks—selling in the market, attending fiestas, or processing foods for sale. Women will send a child to the market to buy a serving of prepared food for whomever wishes to eat at that moment. The lone diner most often will not eat seated at the table but will place the bowl of food on a chair and seat himself on a *butaca* (low curved-back stool)—a traditional Zapotec seat only about six inches off the ground—using the regular chair as a table. One might come into a home almost any hour of the day and find someone seated thus taking a meal. To me, the casual meal pattern typified the culture with its strong emphasis on individualism and independent action. It also was a meal pattern which fit into people's daily lives, where every adult in the family might be coming and going at different times, pursuing their work. An interesting comparison can be made today in the United States where mealtimes are becoming individual as several people in the household work different schedules and frozen food and microwave ovens make meals-in-minutes the rule.

There are a few exceptions to the individualistic meal-taking. In young families when there are children too young to feed themselves, the small family of mother, father, and little ones may eat together squatting around a communal pot of food placed on the floor. The second exception is when there is a guest for a meal and another exception is the communal meals taken at all fiestas, when men and women eat as a group, though separately in shifts.

Besides the crude kitchen table and benches or chairs, the only furnishings in most Zapotec homes are two or three hammocks reserved for adult members and older children, and the sleeping mats on which younger children sleep. Another standard fixture is the household shrine which may be any kind of small table or shelf covered with a white cloth on which flowers, candles, pictures or statues of saints and photographs of deceased family members are placed. There is usually the *baul*, an ornately carved wooden trunk on legs, which contained the woman of the household's dowry when she married. The sum of manufactured furnishings may include a treadle sewing machine, a small radio, and a blender. Doña Lucia, being more prosperous than many, owned two radios, an old portable typewriter nobody ever used, and a small record-player.

Doña Lucia's house was not as easy to clean or as comfortable as the House-on-the-Hill but by now I was more accustomed to the Zapotec way and paid less attention to the inevitable dust and dirt than when I first arrived. I emphasize here that the dirt is not a result of the carelessness and indolence of the Zapotec people as their mestizos neighbors would have one believe, but rather to the conditions under which they live.

The main reason for the dirt in Doña Lucia's house was the traditional roof, consisting of wood slats overlain with mud, on which the roof tiles were laid. Bits of old dried mud fell from the ceiling constantly, making it imperative to keep all pots and containers covered or inverted. The dirt fell on me during the night and I eventually learned to sleep with a handkerchief over my face. A quantity of grit covered the sheet of my cot each morning.

My occupation of the rooms had destroyed the bats' daytime habitat. Ramon took charge of bat eradication every night at dusk by throwing a baseball at the few remaining animals until they flew out the open windows which were then shut for the night.

It was my good fortune to be fond of all forms of wildlife because Doña Lucia's solar was full of it. Besides the bats, there were many little lizards—finger-length creatures which darted up the walls and over the ceilings. Doña Lucia said the spots of urine the lizards left would raise blisters on the skin but I was spared the opportunity to discover this for myself. Pigeons roosted in the roof between the tiles and the wood slats and their family activities rather frequently resulted in feathers floating down with the dried mud. Once during a tremendous windstorm three dead baby pigeons plummeted to the floor of the bathroom, along with the remains of their nest.

I soon learned that I had to be careful to prop the bathroom door shut at night. Otherwise, a barefoot visit in the dark could be enlivened by an encounter with an opossum. I suspected there was some connection between a dense population of oversized cockroaches and the opossums' interest in that particular room. Over all, the place was sort of a miniature zoo and only occasionally did I lose patience over the extra work and inconvenience our faunal housemates caused.

Doña Lucia's house was also extremely inconvenient by U.S. standards because of its decentralized layout. It must have been particularly hard for Chica and even more difficult for her ill mother to do even the barest necessities of food preparation. In order to make a cup of coffee, one had to descend the steep hill at the rear of the house for a piece of firewood, take the coffee container to the opposite far side of the house site to rinse it and fill it under the only water tap outside of the bathroom. This accomplished, one had to search among the clutter of the table for a little paper bag of coffee, the sugar, and a clean spoon, then cross the courtyard to Doña Lucia's quarters to get yesterday's coffee bowls, wash these at the tap, boil and serve the coffee. The final difficulty was that there were uneven paths and floors, foot-high doorsills (to serve as barriers to pigs), obstacles to kick from the pathway while balancing bowls of hot coffee in each hand. Much to everyone's amusement, I was not adept at clearing all the hurdles and frequently stumbled. Knowing the Zapotecs' fondness for appropriate nicknames, I suspected I was known by something like the Zapotec equivalent of "Big Foot" although nobody ever had the bad manners to be so disrespectful in my presence.

There were advantages to living in Doña Lucia's house too. One advantage was that she and I had more time to talk. During the days she was feeling well enough, she spent hours reminiscing, while I listened and encouraged her with questions. And there was also a good deal of activity in her house. Although ill and unable to get out herself, she was anything but isolated from community life. There was a daily flow of persons coming and going. First, in a community without telephones, messages had to be carried by people. Early mornings and evenings after dark were the hours people came on business; to buy an ox team or a pig, to pay for milk they bought yesterday, to solicit orders for tomorrow's tortillas, to deliver a huipil Doña Lucia had ordered a month earlier, to buy maize, or to borrow against a pair of gold earrings. The loans she made on gold jewelry were a bone of contention between her and her son because she charged little or no interest and allowed people almost unlimited time to repay. She did it only as a favor, she said, not to get rich.

Two people, the practical nurse who gave Doña Lucia her insulin shots, and the curandera, came to the house regularly. The shots were supposed to be given daily, but the nurse often did not come. The curandera was sent for when Doña Lucia was feeling particularly ill and decided that it must be more than her health that was troubling her. As a precaution against the evil eye or the envy of her neighbors, she called in the curandera. When one's health continued to deteriorate despite medical doctors, medicines, injections, chest x-rays, and blood transfusions, wasn't it wise to take all precautions, she would ask, knowing that I had much less faith in the native curing than she did.

So the curandera would come to massage her, rub her body with anise-scented alcohol and switch her skin with aromatic nettles. The treatments were rather severe even for a person in good health, I thought, and Doña Lucia sometimes spat blood for several days afterward. I felt she should quit the curandera and she agreed to do so. Then another curandera—the same neighbor whom they had once erroneously suspected of witchcraft against them—came one day and promised Doña Lucia a rapid cure without the heavy massages. This curer diagnosed the trouble as having a supernatural basis and, among other things, advised Doña Lucia to stop eating eggs. Although I did not immediately say so, I was worried about this prohibition because Doña Lucia had few teeth and there were almost no sources of protein other than eggs that she could eat. She did as the curer advised for a week or two but when her health showed no improvement she discontinued the cures.

After I began living in Doña Lucia's house I came to feel more directly the pulse of life in San Juan, to feel myself integrated into the stream of activities, large and small, which constituted people's daily lives. Sometimes I regretted not having moved from Tiu Tono's sooner because I was gaining so many new insights into Zapotec culture in my new home.

Both Doña Lucia and I were avid coffee drinkers. She taught me to make coffee over the three-stone hearth and I soon began boiling coffee for the two of us in the olla each morning and evening, following her instructions. She said I made the best coffee she could remember, and I replied it was because I had such a good teacher. I would rise at dawn (the only really pleasant part of the day) to make the coffee and get ready for the day and we would drink our bowls of coffee and eat the sweet rolls purchased the night before, while sitting in the hammocks. I knew she loved oranges so I began squeezing fresh orange juice for both of us every morning. Later, if I were home when the milk came, I would boil a cup of milk for her, adding a fresh egg and a little sugar. Her spirits rose and she seemed to begin to feel better with my companionship and attention. She began referring to me as *hija* (daughter) and I took to calling her Mamá Lucia instead of the much too formal Doña.

Doña Lucia had a herd of cattle in the countryside and sold milk daily during the short rainy season, the only time that cows gave milk.

A hired man milked the cows each morning in the pasture several miles from the pueblo and sent the milk into town by bus. The tin containing two or three gallons of milk, would arrive at midmorning, dropped by the bus driver in front of Sole's cantina. The servant girl would fetch the tin and then, under Lucia's watchful eye, sell the milk by the liter from the doorway. Milk had to be sold promptly, becoming sour within hours in the heat. Once when the girl did not come, I had to pinch-hit by taking the tin to the street in front of the cantina where I had it all sold in less than an hour. My success probably was due more to the novelty of the gringa selling milk than to my persuasiveness as a saleswoman.

One day Doña Lucia confided that she had her burial clothes made and packed away along with a white sheet for a shroud and a pair of new black sandals. Not long after this an old man arrived one morning with some unfamiliar paraphernalia. He set to work building a little fire in the middle of the courtyard.

"He is a candlemaker," Doña Lucia told me, "Come to make the *velas* (candles) for my funeral."

"Oh, Mamá Lucia," I protested, "You are not going to die! Haven't you been feeling better each day?"

But my automatic and ethnocentric protest was meaningless to her. Of course she was going to die. Everybody did. And it was only the most imprudent person who died without having made preparations. She asked the hired girl to bring her black velvet huipil and her blue lace skirt with white lace flounce from the trunk to show me. All she needed were the candles, and they were going to be made today.

The old man set about his tasks, hanging his candle rack, a wooden wheel-like hoop, from a beam in the roof. At four approximately equidistant points on the hoop he attached the long cords which would serve as the wicks, each of the cords weighted with a small piece of wood to hold it steady as the hot wax was poured over it. A wood basin placed under the rack would catch the excess wax as it dripped from the nascent candles at each pouring. Doña Lucia asked the servant girl to bring out the thirty-plus pounds of beeswax she had purchased several months earlier.

Having lit the fire and set everything in readiness, the candlemaker began his day's work. Seated on a little bench in front of the rack with the pot of melting wax over the fire at his right, he began pouring the hot wax over the wicks, using a half-gourd dipper. At first the work progressed rapidly, one pouring following upon another, but as the candles grew larger the time between pourings became longer and longer. Hurrying the process, explained Doña Lucia, led to candles of poor quality with gulleys and ridges running down their sides. Ah, yes, she knew all about making candles. Many were the candles she had made in her life. But now she did not have the strength to do it.

As the hours spun slowly away into the afternoon, I became impatient with the procedure. I asked Doña Lucia why she did not buy the finished candles I had seen in the markets. Wouldn't that be faster and cheaper? She was aghast.

"Those ugly candles?" she exclaimed incredulously. "Ay, such inferior goods will never cross *my* doorway! Haven't you noticed how dark they are? How small? And all the ridges and irregularities they have?"

The defects of the candles for sale in the markets had eluded my unpracticed eye but I could not bring myself to admit my ignorance.

"Oh, of course, Mamá Lucia, the market candles cannot compare with these beautiful candles the maestro is making for you."

By mid-afternoon the four candles were finished, each about three feet tall and five inches in diameter. As at Tiu Tono's wake, two would burn at Doña Lucia's head and two at her feet on the day she died.

Next day when the candles were thoroughly cooled, she ordered them carefully wrapped in newspaper and stored on the rafters of the ceiling, awaiting the time they would be needed.

13

Que Le Vaya Bien

With the move to my new quarters and the multitude of half-completed tasks that are the inevitable condition of the last few months of fieldwork, I had not taken the time to visit Chica at her own home. I had daily news of her through Anastasio, home on vacation from the mission school and helping his mother make the little house home once again.

Chica was not well, Anastasio reported. She tired easily and spent much time sleeping in the hammock. That was to be expected with the pregnancy and her already less than optimal physical condition, but I worried about her and promised myself daily that I would take the time to visit. Nearly two weeks passed before I finally summoned the time and energy to go over late one afternoon.

The house was near the center of San Juan, a few blocks beyond the marketplace. When I arrived, I was pleased to find Chica cheerful and energetic, bustling around preparing the evening meal in the open-air kitchen. Chica's solar was among the most modest I had seen in San Juan, consisting of a postage-stamp size courtyard and one small dark room with a dirt floor, in front of which was the corredor of equal dimensions. The room had originally been built with two spaces left for the windows facing the street but the spaces had been filled in with loose stacked bricks to keep out intruders, leaving the room always dark. There was no other solution for those who could not afford expensive iron bars and shutters.

Except for a ragged hammock strung on one side of the room and a rope stretched across the opposite side to serve as a clothes rack, there were no furnishings. Another hammock, also faded and torn, hung in the corredor. Anastasio had managed to find an old wood table and a couple of chairs in the storeroom of his aunt's store, and these, along with the two hammocks and two water jars comprised the entire furnishings. There was no piped water but there was electricity, a single bare bulb hanging from a beam of the corredor feebly lighting the area. Anastasio proudly showed me a little dry shower of reeds he had constructed for his mother in one corner of the solar. Here one could bathe in privacy with a small olla of water, a half-gourd dipper, a piece of black soap, and a homegrown luffa sponge.

Anastasio had also built a reed gate to close off the entrance from the street. This kept children, pigs, and dogs out and obscured the occupants from the view of passersby, but provided no security from unwanted visitors. Chica remarked that security was not of much importance anyway because they had nothing worth stealing. I thought at least the smallness of the place was advantageous for her compared to the distances she had had to walk back and forth between faucet, fire, and table at Doña Lucia's. Chica's kitchen area was only a few steps from the corredor and there were not those acres of concrete floors to sweep daily as in the house of her mother. By sprinkling a little water over the dirt floor several times a day, it stayed relatively hard packed and dust free.

Chica was so happy to see me that I felt ashamed I had not come sooner. I was ecstatic to see her in such good spirits. She insisted that I stay for supper and I consented even though I knew she probably had barely enough food for the three of them. Still I could not risk hurting her pride by offering to go to the market to buy more.

The meal was simple—boiled rice seasoned with chile and onions, a handful of dried shrimp, a sliver of dry cheese, and tortillas she had made herself. I tried to eat very little so that Cata would have something when he came home but at the same time I could not let her suspect my motives. Actually I ate more than I intended. Chica was an excellent cook and could make the simplest dish appetizing by adding a pinch of herb or a clove of garlic. She apologized because there was no coffee. I knew this was a great embarrassment to her because she was aware of my love for boiled coffee but I tried to be the perfect guest, saying I understood because I could never endure the smell of coffee either when I was pregnant.

We were almost finished eating when Cata arrived. He had been drinking and was in a state of euphoria but still self-contained and well in control of his actions. He greeted me politely and sat down at the table. Chica placed a bowl of rice before him.

"And so, my dearest wife," he began, "why didn't you speak to me when I called to you as you passed Pedro's cantina?"

A cloud of rage darkened Chica's face, rising out of the depths of her suffering with all the suddenness of a summer thunderstorm.

"I? Speak to you, you drunken bastard? Oh, you have no shame! Sitting in the cantina all day when you should be out trying to earn a few pesos to support your family! Look at us, with no money, no food on the table, and you, *you* creature who calls himself a man, *you dare to ask why I do not speak to you*!"

The vehemence of the outburst startled me. I knew she was angry but I had never seen her so overcome with rage. Except for the quarrel over my seat coming home from San Marcos, I had never heard Chica raise her voice. I had often seen her hurt and sad but never angry, save for that one quarrel on my behalf. Now she seemed to have forgotten my presence. A rapid stream of Zapotec, only some of it intelligible to me, rolled off her tongue like bullets from a machine gun. Anastasio was embarrassed. To ease the situation he and I began to talk to each other of something else. I remained perhaps fifteen minutes more, talking with Anastasio about his school, life in Veracruz, anything to keep us distracted. I waited for Chica to stop her tongue-lashing so I could graciously take my leave.

Cata responded to her verbal assault with utter silence, passively staring at his bowl. Perhaps he was waiting until I left, or maybe the alcohol was beginning to stupefy him. At length—when it seemed that Chica would not, could not, stop scolding—I left quietly, Anastasio seeing me to the gate.

Walking home in the dusk, I tried to gather my thoughts. Here was a facet of Chica I had seen only a hint of before. I could understand her rage at Cata after his thousand promises over the years to quit drinking. Yet she had seemed almost out of control—to the point of self-destruction.

Over the years since, I have thought a great deal about Chica and about anthropologists and their "key informants." A special relationship often develops between an anthropologist and one or more key informants, that is closer than those the anthropologist generally develops in her home country. Perhaps this is because in the field, the anthropologist is dependent on the key informant for so many things—information, rules of behavior, how to get out of a cultural jam, or how to cook on three stones. More significantly, the anthropologist is dependent on key informants for friendship and moral support.

It is a reciprocal relationship. The key informant also has to find satisfaction in the relationship—whether a sense of friendship and closeness to the outsider that is lacking in the home community, a sense of importance for being useful as a kind of teacher to a naive visitor, or some other intangible. Key informants may be paid for their time but I doubt that money is ever their primary reason for maintaining the relationship. Usually persons who volunteer to help the fieldworker are persons who are somehow not entirely integrated into their own culture. Perhaps they feel themselves outsiders, having been born elsewhere, as was probably the case with my compadre, Leonzo. Perhaps they feel different and unaccepted for some physical attribute, or they have a sense of only partly belonging—of being on the fringes of their society for some other reason. This detachment, whatever its source, is what makes them so valuable to the anthropologist because it allows the informant to look at her own culture with something of the eye of an outside observer, and to see and explain aspects of the culture which others would not perceive.

When Chica wept that even her family did not respect her, she was voicing a shadow of the truth. I am sure her family loved her greatly but most of the things which counted for respect in San Juan had somehow eluded her. She was not wealthy, she was a successful mother only two out of ten tries, she did not protect herself from an abusive husband, she had been unsuccessful at past market ventures (trading in fish) and was physically not strong enough to endure the long hours of travel and market-selling through which most wives earn an income. She was too poor to attend many fiestas much less sponsor them, and, worse still, she had sent her two sons away to a Protestant missionary school. Though most of her neighbors and relatives liked her as a person, they probably considered her a failure as a woman.

The attributes which had endeared her to me were her intelligence, her honesty, integrity, pride, loyalty to friends and family, and her generosity. Chica had a soft heart for every hapless creature and every human being with a hard-luck story. Objects of her sympathy were never difficult to find. When she had money it slipped through her fingers to help other people—a loan to a neighbor, a little gift for her mother, a plate of food for the paraplegic man who lived for a time under a tree near the market. In the hard-scrabble existence of San Juan, Chica's characteristics were not those greatly admired by most of the inhabitants, however noble they may seem to us from our comfortable, far-removed lives. Perhaps in another culture where her personality traits were more valued she would have found a more satisfying life, but it was not to be. I recall Margaret Mead once describing the tragedy of a native informant as a "natural scientist" born into an uncurious culture. Chica was a "natural caregiver" born into a culture which valued other less altruistic attributes. The cruelest blow of all, she was denied by nature the opportunity to share that generosity and bountiful love with her own children.

* * *

As the time for me to leave neared, Doña Lucia began to fret about my trip home.

"But how will you find your way all alone?" she asked.

I got out the road map and showed her where we were and where California was. I traced my route, naming the cities I would pass through and relating details of the topography along the way.

"Here at Tepić," I explained, pointing my finger, "the highway comes down steeply off the big mesa that makes up all of central Mexico and then the coast appears. After that, all the way to California it will be coastal desert, dry and sandy."

I pointed out places where there were shrines she might have heard about and towns where something historical had happened during the Revolution, a time remembered from her girlhood.

"And how many days will it take you to get to California?"

"I'm not sure but I think I can make it in five or six days. I don't like to drive long hours or after dark because I am alone so I won't travel as fast as if there were another person to help drive."

"But I still do not understand how you know what road to take," she insisted. "Look, there are many roads on this map. How do you know to take one and not the others?"

"Oh, but it's very easy, Mamá Lucia. All I have to do is just read the signs. All the roads have numbers and destinations and I simply stay on the road which has the number that takes me to the next large town on the way to California. After passing through a city there will be another road sign stating next city destination and giving the number of the road. I look on the map to make sure that is the road number that will take me to California. With the help of the map, I can always find out just where I am in the journey. So don't worry, I won't get lost."

Doña Lucia sighed with relief. She had never understood how I had been able to find my way to San Juan alone and now at last she understood. As for herself, she said, she had a great fear of getting lost. She began relating how she had once become lost in Oaxaca. It was the most terrifying experience of her life, and since then she was always afraid of getting lost if she left San Juan.

A few evenings before my departure, Chica arrived as I was packing items I would no longer need into the camper. She was followed by a boy carrying something heavy and bulky, shrouded in cloth.

"This is for you to remember us by when you are faraway in your home," she announced.

She removed the coverings and there stood a perfect little half-sized *tinajera*, the traditional three-piece water jar with stand shaped like a woman holding a water jar on her head. She had ordered it made especially for me because I had mentioned that I would not have room to carry a regular four-foot-tall tinajera. I was very touched by her thoughtfulness and her generosity when she had scarcely enough to feed her family—yet I was not at all surprised by this gesture, so typical of her. Chica was always thinking of others, giving to others, and helping others. Her generous nature was surely a deciding factor when she extended her hand in friendship and invited me, a stranger, to the fiesta that first day we met.

Just before my departure date, the biggest wedding in years was to take place. It would be a traditional Zapotec wedding—the groom's entourage taking the prescribed gifts of chickens, a young bull, a goat, a bag of seed corn, and other items to the bride's parents beforehand—something that had not been seen in years. They would return with the bride's wedding trunk filled with her dowry of gold jewelry and clothing.

The family of Doña Lucia was all abustle with excitement and activity because the bridegroom-to-be was Magda's stepson. Although he and his bride-to-be lived in Mexico City, they had requested a traditional ceremony in San Juan. I delayed my return to California for a week in order to participate in this important event.

As Chica and Doña Lucia became involved in the wedding preparations, both seemed much improved in body and spirit. Chica was still in full mourning for a comadre but this did not deter her from helping with the preparations. The opportunity to be an intimate part of such a magnificent fiesta as this wedding comes but rarely in one's life. Chica, Doña Lucia, and Faustina all had certain specific obligations in the way of duties and food contributions and even I was included as a "daughter" in Doña Lucia's home.

Several days before the wedding, women began bringing supplies to Magda's house. Doña Lucia, being the maternal grandmother (in a social sense) of the groom, was expected to bring a kilogram of *cacao* (cocoa beans), ten fresh eggs and a live chicken, as well as two kilograms of sugar. Other close female relatives, including me, were obligated to bring ten eggs, half a kilogram of cacao, and one live chicken. Distant relatives and neighbors had only to give five eggs and perhaps a little cacao if they could afford it. People try to exceed the amount of the minimum requirements, the idea being to make the best showing possible within prescribed limits. Doña Lucia actually donated twenty eggs and two kilograms of cacao in addition to the other items.

The whole week preceding the wedding found Doña Lucia at Magda's house from early morning until long after dark. During the first days she left her own house each morning about 7:00 a.m. to catch the first bus that stopped directly in front of Magda's house. Although Magda's was only about six or seven blocks away, it was too far for the frail Doña Lucia to walk. We usually went together but if I was not ready Doña Lucia impatiently left without me. Toward the last of the week, as the wedding day approached, Doña Lucia no longer returned home at night but slept in a hammock in her daughter's corredor. She was in a great state of excitement and, even though she spent most of the days lying in the hammock, it was obvious that her frail health was under a heavy strain. But nothing short of death could have kept Doña Lucia away from the wedding activities. For nearly two years she had been in such poor health that she could seldom leave her home. At Magda's house she was able to see and visit with old friends and acquaintances she had not seen for years, and I think she knew she would not see again.

Sunday marks the day of weddings in San Juan, beginning with an 8:00 a.m. mass at the church. On the preceding Thursday a group of women gather at a neighbor's house to make the *marquesote*, a traditional part of every fiesta. Marquesote is a sponge cake and as such uses quantities of fresh eggs. The task requires the efforts of twenty or so women for most of the day and is held in the house and under the direction of a neighbor hired as a specialist to oversee the cakemaking. The eggs, many dozens of them, were beaten manually with wooden beaters and the cakes baked in clay pots in outdoor wood-fired ovens of the beehive construction.

For my research on women's economic roles, I was trying to keep track of all the expenses and contributions of the wedding, but there were so many eggs used that I lost track—except to note that two washtubs of eggs in the shell were used in the making of the marquesote. Later I measured the capacity of a washtub and the space a dozen eggs required to arrive at a reasonably accurate estimate of the number of eggs used.

The whole affair of the marquesote was charged with tension because of the degree of risk involved in baking sponge cake under such uncontrolled conditions and the scale of the operation. If something went awry—the eggs underbeaten, insufficient flour added, the oven temperature too high or too low—the cakes would fall to the flatness and consistency of pancakes and would not serve for fiesta food. For this reason, a certain amount of ritual and magic go along with making marquesote. One of these rituals was the stringing of the empty eggshells into necklaces which the participants wore around their necks while they worked.

There was also a traditional *pito y tambor* (flute and drum) ensemble in attendance playing ancient Zapotec melodies. This was one of only a handful of ritual occasions when the old Zapotec instruments and music were played. When the cakes had baked satisfactorily and were ready to distribute, a colorful procession of the two musicians, the host household's members, the marquesote makers, and the young women who would deliver it emerged into the street to the ear-shattering explosions of fireworks, the announcement that the baking had been a success. The cakes would be distributed to each woman who brought a contribution of eggs, to each one who helped with the baking, to all the invited wedding guests, and to all those who would be bringing contributions of food and money during the festivities.

Saturday was the day to bring chickens. All day long women came to Magda's house—the live hens, with legs bound, hanging upside down over one arm. The chickens were received one by one in the corredor. Each bird, decorated with red ribbons and a large red flower, was admired and accepted by Chica, her mother, or other family member. The donor was then seated and given hot chocolate, a sweet roll, and marquesote. Red, rather than white, is the color for weddings, symbolizing the wish for virginity and later fertility for the bride. After the marriage is consummated, it is the color red that announces to the public that the bride was indeed a virgin and all is well.

About 6:00 p.m. the chicken deliveries stepped up as the last call, a series of firecrackers set off in the street, announced to townspeople that the chickens must be delivered immediately. The birds still had to be killed, cleaned, and cooked for the wedding feast the next day—a monumental task which would require many hands and most of the night. In all, seventy-eight chickens were donated and prepared for the wedding feast, but these were only a small part of the meat requirements for the affair. The groom's father also purchased two oxen and three large pigs, all of them butchered, cooked, and consumed during the three-day celebration.

For months I had been concerned about Chica's welfare after I left the field. I had kept a careful record of the time she had helped me and of the various small "loans" I had made her. I owed her a few thousand pesos still, since she had refused repeatedly to take anything resembling pay. At first, I planned to hand the sum to her as a wrapped gift when I bade her goodbye and ask her not to open it until after I left, but Chica's generous nature and soft heart made such a plan impractical. She would let the money slip through her fingers long before the baby was born—loaning here, giving there as she always did when she had any cash. I wanted her to have some security at the baby's birth so that there would be no reason for not performing the caesarean section the doctor thought might be needed. After much thought, I decided the best way would be to invest the cash in a gold coin necklace which she could sell or pawn if and when an emergency occurred.

On the pretext that I wanted the jewelry for myself, I had given Chica the money some weeks earlier and she and Faustina had ordered the piece from the *platero* (jewelry maker). I asked her to order what she thought was the most beautiful piece for the money since I knew little about gold coins, length of chains, and styles and was not a good judge of quality or workmanship. The result was a striking pendant necklace made from a large gold coin called a *centenario*. When it was delivered to me, we all admired it before I packed it away to await the day of my departure when I would slip it quietly into her hand at the last minute. I told nobody of my plan, wanting to keep the gift a surprise.

As the wedding date approached I began to think it would be best to give Chica the necklace before the wedding so she could wear it during the important occasion when other women were displaying their gold jewelry. Chica owned only a small pair of gold earrings and I imagined how delighted she would be to wear this magnificent necklace. Mourning attire, while grim, does not preclude the wearing of a respectable amount of gold jewelry. At this point it seemed best to ask Doña Lucia's advice. Her reaction was not what I expected.

"Oh, no! You can't handle it that way, hija. That won't do at all!" she protested when I mentioned that I just wanted to hand the necklace to Chica in private.

"Why not?"

"Why not? *Why not*? Ay, mi hija, *you* know how jealous Cata is. If you give her the necklace in private he will accuse her of receiving it from a paramour. It will cause all manner of trouble."

Here was a whole new perspective I had not even considered, but a moment's reflection told me that Doña Lucia was right.

"Well, what shall we do then?" I asked.

"*Mira*, here's what we must do. We must give the necklace to her in front of Cata with Pedro (Magda's husband) acting as a witness so that Cata cannot wrongly accuse her some time later when you and I are not here to remind him of the facts. I will speak to Pedro about it tomorrow and let you know when to present the necklace."

Now, twenty-three years later, I see another solution where I saw none at the time. I could have told Chica I was loaning my necklace to her, as women often do, just to wear for the fiesta, and still could have given it to her privately before I left. That way Cata and the family would have been aware of its source and potential trouble averted without the public spectacle of a formal presentation which promised to be everything I did not want.

When the small ceremony occurred Saturday afternoon in Magda's corredor I was embarrassed because it appeared to me as if I were trying to be the bountiful fairy godmother, when in fact Chica had earned the necklace and more. Chica seemed embarrassed too and the whole affair seemed in poor taste, repulsively "ugly American." I regretted that I had not insisted on paying her regularly from the start.

The wedding ceremonies and festivities lasted for three days and nights. While not in continuous attendance, I took copious notes on the "wedding of the decade," which added to my insights into the importance of the ritual exchanges of goods and money in the fiesta system.

A couple of days before I was to leave, friends and neighbors began arriving with gifts for me even though I thought I had made it clear that I would not have space to take much of anything extra with me. Generously, my friends came with stacks of totopos, pieces of hard cheese, salted shrimp, a small package of ground coffee, and even a live chicken. They did not want me to be hungry on the long trip home.

The day before I left San Juan, word came that Chica was having difficulty walking and had not been out of the house since the wedding. It was near sundown when I made my way through the dusty streets to her house to bid her goodbye. She was sitting on a log that partially blocked the entrance looking very dejected in her black mourning, waiting for me. Seating myself on the log beside her, we talked. I gave her a two-month supply of vitamins and told her I had paid Dr. Mario for the injections still needed to finish the series. Trying my best to be cheerful and upbeat while I felt frightened for her and sad, I reiterated that I was certain if she did what the doctor advised everything would turn out all right. Then next summer I would be the madrina of the new baby, bringing its clothes for baptism all the way from California. Dusk was descending rapidly as we embraced one last time and kissed each other's cheeks. As I walked away down the narrow street with a heavy heart, I could feel her eyes following me.

The next morning, in the clammy, almost chilly predawn hours of mid-November I left San Juan—the pick-up less loaded than when

I came but still stuffed with books, sheafs of field notes, farewell gifts, and the miscellaneous items I had acquired. Doña Lucia, Sole, and Ramon all insisted on rising to bid me goodbye. Doña Lucia, shaking with a chill, weeping, and coughing, seemed as fragile as a dry November leaf. I wept too for I knew it would be a miracle if Doña Lucia lived to see my return.

Ramon cranked up his old jalopy and followed me the few miles out to the highway, his uncertain headlights blinking and winking in my rearview mirror. I was counting on Ramon to keep me informed of events by letter and I hoped he would keep his promise. At the highway intersection we honked and waved as I drove away toward California.

14
The Last Goodbye

Once back in California, urgencies descended on me like a cloud of San Juan sancudos. I set about preparing and writing my dissertation, anxious to finish before my limited funds were exhausted. The days flew by as I worked feverishly on my final student task.

Ramon kept his promise, sending a few short notes saying everyone was doing as well as expected. Anastasio wrote once from the mission school in Veracruz. I heard from my comadre Alberta and from my compadres Leonzo and Jonsa in reply to a note I had sent announcing my safe arrival. Their letters tended to be the stiff, formal Spanish equivalent of the we-are-fine-how-are-you variety that conveyed little news.

It was difficult to believe that I found myself so thoroughly homesick for my friends in San Juan. Everything about California seemed strange to me—the mountains flatter, the women more grotesquely made up, the new miniskirt styles incredibly ugly, the people excessively pale with inordinately large noses, and the traffic simply unreal. Within a few weeks I was involved in two fender-benders that were my fault because I could not seem to handle all the assaults on my sensory facilities. I felt like a stranger in my own country. Although I did not recognize it at the time, I was suffering from culture-shock in reverse. I recovered completely only after perhaps two years.

In late February a note came from Ramon with the sad news that Chica's baby, a girl, had been stillborn. This was the *ninth* child she had lost. I imagined how defeated she felt by her latest loss. The good news was that Chica was fine and had not needed a caesarian section. That Chica had fared so well was such good news, despite the baby's death, that I gave an audible little cheer while reading the letter at my mailbox, causing a passerby to give me a surprised glance. I wrote Chica a long letter of condolence, full of plans for the coming summer. I wanted her to come back to California with me for a few weeks and I was already beginning to make arrangements. I knew she would be excited and pleased, and hoped that the anticipation would take her mind from her most recent loss.

Only a few days later I was deeply saddened, though not surprised, by a terse note from Ramon saying Doña Lucia had died suddenly from a heart attack. I went to the church near my home, lit candles, and prayed for her in the manner of her culture.

The mourning period for Doña Lucia would be difficult for Chica coming so soon after the birth. Besides the sense of profound sadness that always comes when one's mother dies, she would be expected to spend nine days in heavy mourning, much of it kneeling and praying with the others in front of the household shrine. By telegram I sent two hundred pesos to buy flowers and extra candles for the funeral.

There was no telephone in San Juan, telegraph was uncertain, and mail went at a snail's pace. I did not hear anything about the funeral or if the money was received.

In April a letter from Ramon mentioned that Chica had a bad cough, contracted, he thought, during the forty-day anniversary mass for their mother. Knowing Chica, I was certain she was not caring for herself properly and had probably worked far too hard in preparations for the mixa gue'tu'. I wrote admonishing her to take care of herself and sent a money order for a hundred pesos in case she should need medicine. I did not expect a response. If she wanted to send a letter, she would have to wait until Anastasio came home on vacation to write it for her. Ramon's letters were getting fewer and shorter too. It was so difficult to keep in touch over such distances by uncertain mail.

May third dawned as my red-letter day, the day I had worked for and anticipated for five long years. The first draft of the dissertation was finished and I had an appointment that morning at the university. At 8:00 a.m. I was on campus waiting in the office of the chairman of my doctoral committee to hand the document to him personally. It was almost like handing over my own child, so much of me and the past few years of my life were bound up in that manuscript.

It was already dark that evening when I returned home. Stopping at the mailbox I was surprised but pleased to see an envelope from Chica! Anastasio must be home on vacation, I thought. Tearing it open with eager anticipation, I read it in the dim light of the street lamp:

> My Valued and Dearest Friend:
>
> I write this with much sadness as I must tell you that my mother is very ill and she thinks she will not get well again. My mamá loves you very much and wishes she could see you. When you come, I hope she is well again. Receive from my mamá this strong embrace and kiss which she sends. My mother tells you goodbye.
>
> Sincerely,
> Anastasio

"Oh, my God!" I cried. I thought perhaps I had misread the letter in the dim light of the street. I ran home and read it again. No mistake, it said just what I had understood. Was I having a bad dream? Chica was dying? It must be a bad dream, I thought. Soon I will wake up to find it is not true.

Tears coursing down my cheeks, I picked up the telephone. I would send a telegram to Ramon telling him I could come right away, tomorrow even, if he thought I should. Sending the telegram made me feel a little better. He should have it by morning and I might have an answer sometime tomorrow. I called the airline, packed a small bag, and waited.

I awaited his reply all the interminable following day, then the next, the next, and the next. The wait was agonizing but I comforted myself with the thought that probably Chica was improving. Otherwise, Ramon would surely have sent an answer to my telegram. Then on the fifth day the mailman brought a *letter* from Ramon.

When I saw it I felt reassured that it held good news. Otherwise why would he send word the slowest way? I tore open the envelope with trembling fingers.

> Dear Señora:
>
> It is with profound sadness that I inform you my sister, Francisca, died this morning at 9:00 a.m.
>
> Ramon

Oh, my God! Oh, my God! Chica!

The rest of that day is a blur but I remember that I sat at the breakfast table and wept for a long, long time.

Days later while once again reading the two letters, now dog-eared from so many readings, I noticed for the first time the date on the postmark of Ramon's heart-breaking note. It was May 3—that same day which had begun with the submission of my doctoral dissertation draft, had ended with the arrival of Chica's devastating farewell letter. Even now, twenty-four years later, reliving those tragic days while editing this book brings tears to my eyes.

PART II

Returnings

15

Returnings: 1968-1975

The summer of 1968 remains a blur. I returned to San Juan for Chica's mixa que'tu', postponed until July so that I could attend. During the weeks I was there that summer, I saw San Juan in shades of gray—every street, every nook of Doña Lucia's house, and every encounter with other friends and informants brought painful memories of Chica and Doña Lucia. I wondered if I would ever be able to pick up the pieces and continue research here again.

My return to California that summer found me even more estranged from my own culture than on my first return a few months earlier. I needed to share the grief with someone but there was nobody else who knew the culture and the people—nobody who could share the deep suffering in my heart. It was comforting to be reunited with my two children but even that long dreamed of pleasure was dampened by how much both they and I had changed in the fifteen months of my absence. We had to become reacquainted and that required time and patience. I seemed unable to pull myself out of depression over the deaths of my friends and, in retrospect, probably also because I wondered if my children and I would ever be as close as we were before the fieldwork. Happily, we did reestablish our parent-child relationship, at least to my satisfaction, within a few months.

In response to the emptiness I felt and the compulsion to share my experiences, I wrote the first version of *La Zandunga*. The writing brought solace and served as the catharsis I needed. When it was done, my depression began to lift. I completed the first year of teaching full time, then the second, while my thoughts turned back more and more to my dissertation. Although it was completed to the satisfaction of the university and I had been awarded the doctoral degree, I was not satisfied with it as a description of Isthmus Zapotec culture, focusing as it did so heavily on women's economic roles. There was so much more to Zapotec culture and women's lives than the monograph conveyed. How could I explain an aspect of Zapotec culture which had been called matriarchy when that was so definitely wrong, yet describe the fine nuances of the egalitarian milieu in which men and women interacted?

For a year I thought about the problem, reviewing my field notes and airing my ideas in the classroom. The intellectual revolution in the social sciences brought about by the Women's Movement was brewing but had not yet seen the light of publication. At professional meetings women were discussing problems with the traditional anthropological approach to gender roles—one centered so unilaterally on men. I began to have doubts about the accuracy of the whole body of published ethnographies. Were the Isthmus Zapotecs truly so unique or were there many other cultures where women and women's roles and gender interactions simply had not been investigated sufficiently to give us the full picture?

Poring over field notes night after night I realized how much data I had recorded on women's nonformal roles and behavior which did not fit into the standard ethnographic pattern of the time, yet constituted the essence of what I saw as the basis of Isthmus Zapotec women's power and equality. More searching the anthropological sources, more thought, and more pondering finally led to the formulation of a model of gender roles by which I thought it would be possible to explain women's central place in Isthmus Zapotec culture.

What this experience demonstrated to me was the absolute necessity of recording as far as possible everything observed, heard, and elicited while in the field, even when the data seemed entirely irrelevant to the research focus. No ethnographer can record everything, of course, but the closer one comes to that goal the richer with cultural data the field notes will be.

During 1970-1971, I restructured the dissertation into *The Isthmus Zapotecs: Women's Roles in Cultural Context*, published in 1973. With the added emphasis on women's roles outside an economic context I felt I had finally captured on paper—in a way I hoped would be understandable to readers—something of Isthmus Zapotec gender relations.

Although I continued to return to San Juan for a few weeks almost every summer, it was not until 1975 that I was able to carry out a whole new project on other aspects of the culture that interested me. During the interim summers, I had become closer to Chica's sisters, my comadre Faustina and Magda, whom I had not known well earlier. Before Doña Lucia died, Faustina had moved back into the family home with her baby to take care of her mother. Afterward she did not return to her in-laws but continued to live on in her natal home, and eventually divorced her husband. On my summer visits I stayed there too, making my yearly transitions from California to San Juan much easier because my supplies—typewriter, electric fan, cot, and office furniture—could be left in the house between visits.

Two subjects interested me: family nutrition, and traditional midwives and births. I made plans to investigate both during the one-semester leave in 1975. The research plan called for hiring and training one or two local helpers to assist in observing and collecting data about family eating patterns.

I had no idea who I might find to help with the research but I would definitely need someone immediately—particularly to help with setting up interviews to explain my project to potential participating families. Betina was now teaching school full time and had two more children. Several other people I approached were also otherwise occupied. Then Faustina suggested Tivi, our neighbor whom I occasionally bought food from in 1967 and who had, on occasion, acted as a casual informant.

Tivi was a good prospective helper for a couple of reasons: 1) She needed income, and 2) She was pregnant with her eighth child and therefore an ideal informant for a birth/midwife project.

Supporting a sporadically-employed husband and five living children, the thirty-two-year-old Tivi was struggling mightily to keep the family economically afloat by selling iguana in mole and other prepared game dishes each morning in the street market at the far end of the pueblo.

Tivi, like most women her age in San Juan, was completely unschooled. Her husband, with just enough schooling to enable him to read and write, apparently felt it was sufficient to make *campesino* (farmhand) day labor beneath him and spent most of his time "looking for" and "waiting for" a job more suited to his education. The family was landless but, through the amazing energy and gargantuan efforts of Tivi and her fourteen-year-old daughter, by 1975 they had managed to purchase a small solar where they lived in a very small choza of the family's own construction.

As difficult as it is to imagine, by 1975 things were actually looking up for Tivi's family. Several years earlier their fortunes had sunk so low that they were homeless and starving. As the only daughter in a very poor, motherless family living in a cramped solar with several brothers and an alcoholic father, Tivi could seek no support for her husband and children from her family. Her husband's family was not helpful because they had opposed the union from the first. Between 1968 and 1973, homelessness and malnutrition contributed to the deaths of two little daughters, aged one and three, within a single six-month period. Shortly after this, Faustina reported, she felt so sorry for her childhood friend that she had opened her solar to the family where they lived rent-free for several months.

Tivi was a pretty woman with a mop of thick curly hair and a dimpled chin and, in spite of her difficult existence, she had an extraordinary knack for seeing and finding humor in the ironies of life. As she often said when a job expectation for her husband fell through or one of her few pigs died, "I might as well laugh about it. I can't change anything."

Needing money (and I prefer to think also because she liked me), Tivi agreed to help. She would explain in Zapotec what I was trying to do and make appointments with women who agreed to talk with us. We would go to the interview together, she acting as translator-interpreter (the same method used in earlier fieldwork). I still did not trust my comprehension of Zapotec enough to rely on it although I could follow the general gist of conversations. We agreed on a rate of pay per interview and she tried to work an interview per day into her busy schedule.

Even after years of difficult living and repeated pregnancies, Tivi was blessed with good health. When informants all too often related histories of diabetes and its complications during our interviews, Tivi would quip: "*Pues*, I don't have sugar (the common name for diabetes), what I have is salt!" And, indeed, if salt is pluck, to be sure she had it.

We began with the nutrition project, which called for recording the amount and kinds of food eaten by each member of the family daily. In a scientifically impeccable study, that would entail weighing each serving of food as well as analyzing it for various elements (fat, carbohydrates, and protein). I knew from the outset that that sort of flawless research would not be possible in San Juan with its illiterate and nutritionally unsophisticated population. But I wanted to do the nutrition study because I suspected different members of the families consumed quite different amounts of essential food elements and that younger children especially were short-changed on nutrition because their mothers did not understand the nutritional needs of the weanling. By collecting the food intake data, I hoped to learn what toddlers were actually consuming and to demonstrate to the mothers what their children's diets were lacking. Most of the needed food elements were readily accessible in the local markets but were not offered to small children because mothers did not know of the child's requirements nor of palatable ways to prepare vitamin-rich vegetables and fruits so that little ones would eat them.

The research plan was to ask family members to recall each evening what they ate that day, then estimate sizes of servings. Nutritional values could be analyzed and recorded later. A flaw in the research plan was that mothers would have to keep track of and report on children under the age of ten, and this placed an impossible task on mothers with several small children. Not being accustomed to paying much attention to what they ate, adults could usually only recall their last meal and then often not specifics such as the number of tortillas consumed. Another major problem was that family members usually do not eat communal meals and that snacking, a substantial contribution to total food intake, occurs throughout the day and is not confined to the home. Even though I was aware of these possible difficulties, I underestimated the degree of difficulty that would arise from a study which depended on informants to remember and report food intake. After a couple of weeks of attempts at getting something resembling accurate data, I reluctantly decided the project was a lost cause.

We then turned our attention to midwives and traditional birth. Tivi was familiar with all the midwives in the pueblo and their reputations, having used the services of two or three in her past births. She thus made an excellent preliminary informant about traditional birth practices and midwives.

San Juan was home to eight practicing *parteras* (midwives) in 1975, all but two of whom had taken at least a government sponsored workshop in aseptic procedures and modern techniques. I had become aware over the years that induced abortion, although illegal, was available to desperate women and thought perhaps more information about it would surface during the course of our work. Very little did in view of the fact that the practice was illegal and clandestine, but women knew where to go for induced abortions in San Juan even though they did not wish to identify the individuals who performed them. Tivi herself confessed that during one of her pregnancies she had been on her way to the abortionist when she met a friend in the street who talked to her about the risks and advised against it. She turned around and went home.

Leonora, Tivi's partera, proved to be one of the most sought-after and popular midwives (as well as the most traditional) in San Juan, occasionally delivering from two to four babies in a twenty-four-hour period. She spoke only Zapotec and had almost no formal training in her profession but I quickly discerned why she was so popular. Leonora was a happy, calm, motherly person of about fifty-five years, who led a simple traditional life with her campesino husband. She exuded an air of friendliness and good will.

Leonora took her work very seriously because she considered it a God-given talent she was "called" to follow. The people of San Juan believe that unless one has the inborn *valor* (courage) midwifery requires, one cannot learn the profession. Serving her apprenticeship under her own mother when she was a young married woman, Leonora had delivered San Juan babies for thirty years, and was proudest of the fact that she had never lost a child or a mother. Part of this good fortune was because difficult cases were always referred to a licensed medical doctor, but it was still an outstanding record.

Leonora's mother—seventy-seven years old and nearly blind—like her daughter, exuded "good vibes." When my question as to when she retired was translated to her, she laughed and replied that she was not retired but had delivered a baby the previous day "with the help of my eyes," indicating a young woman seated nearby. She did not go out on cases anymore except when nobody else was available in emergency situations.

The new San Juan mother does not leave the solar for eight days after the birth, and for people living close to subsistence level it may be difficult for the family to feed themselves for that period without the mother's earnings. Family and neighbors might bring in a small serving or two of food at irregular intervals but it is not enough to feed a large family. Tivi was working far too hard for her own health in order to save up a small sum to feed her five children while she was confined. She was worried about the birth and had a premonition, which proved unfounded, that she might die.

On the morning of the birth, the midwife Leonora was sent for and Tivi's husband, Juan, did not leave the solar. Zapotec husbands are essential to the propitious outcome of a birth. They help support the mother in a half-reclining position, give encouragement and solace and, after the birth, carry out the very important task of placing the placenta in a new pottery jar which is then sealed and buried under the floor of the house. If this task is botched, it is said that the baby's eyes will become infected. Tivi's baby, her fifth son, arrived healthy and robust and did not develop an eye infection.

We resumed our interviewing when the new baby was about twelve days old. Tivi would leave the baby for an hour or so with her eldest daughter, age fifteen. The two-year-old, Nino, was continually whining and had the extended belly of malnutrition. I worried that he had been weaned too soon and mentioned to Tivi that he should be getting more fruit and eggs. There was no fresh milk except during the short rainy season and powdered milk was far too expensive for most families. To placate him when we left each day, Tivi would promise to bring him an orange. The first time this occurred, we were almost home when I suddenly recalled her promise.

"Mira," I said, "we have to go back to the market. We forgot Nino's orange."

"Oh, never mind," she laughed, "He knows I never bring him anything."

On subsequent days I remembered to bring back some piece of fruit for Nino. In San Juan, life was toughest for two-year-olds. The new fashion was to wean early, shortly after one year, while bottle-feeding was still very rare. As a result there were few foods toddlers could eat. Often they seemed to survive on little more than maize gruel, bits of tortillas, bananas, and the liquid from the soup pot. Many of these little tykes did not make it to school age. Weakened by malnutrition, a bout of gastroenteritis from impure water could dehydrate them so severely and so rapidly that they might die in just a few hours. Simple remedies could prevent these deaths but frequently mothers waited too long to consult the doctor. Happily this did not happen to Nino who grew up to be a tall, handsome young man with a dazzling smile.

During 1975 we interviewed all eight midwives, several curers, and over thirty married women under thirty-five, women who were still capable of having more children. We found that most mothers had more children than the three to four they considered ideal. I knew women were interested in birth control. Even in 1966 women had asked me how to prevent pregnancy. Contraceptive pills were already available though rarely used. In 1975, most women were still not using contraceptive pills but that did not mean they were not limiting family size. One thirty-two-year-old mother of five stated emphatically that she was not going to have any more children. When I asked how she would prevent it, she laughed heartily and replied, "Pues, that's not difficult. Just separate the cow from the bull!" Thus I learned that women considered abstinence a reliable, if not always practical, method of limiting family size.

In the United States one often hears "experts" talking about the role of the Catholic Church in maintaining high birth rates in Latin America. In San Juan where everyone considers themselves Catholic by birth, women are unconcerned about church doctrine and do what they feel is necessary for the best chances of their own survival and that of their families. No one ever mentioned the teachings of the Church as a reason for not limiting family size.

In 1975 it was much easier to take pictures than in 1966-67 perhaps because people were more accustomed to my presence and trusted me. I walked around the pueblo openly carrying my camera without people either covering their faces or becoming hostile. People seemed to be more open to outside influences. A few people had television sets which brought glimpses of the larger world, although the world seen on television was certainly not a very accurate portrayal of the actual wider world. Still, television did open people's minds to the possibilities of other lifestyles.

My interest in getting vital statistics from the municipio offices had not diminished since 1967, nor had I been successful. During the 1975 fieldwork I promised myself I would put strenuous effort into viewing the records because figures on child and infant mortality would be very useful to the study. So I began pursuing ways to gain permission to see the records early in the fieldwork. As the following letter to our university department secretary indicates, I was eventually successful, to a degree. The letter also makes clear why anthropologists must spend many months in the field in order to accomplish the goals they set for themselves.

Dear Alice and Department:

Just received the Halazon. Thanks a million. Now I can have more fresh produce. It takes five tablets to purify a small head of leaf lettuce. Since I have been out of the tablets for a few weeks, my mouth is already anticipating *lettuce*!

Yesterday, having tried for several weeks to get a peep at the *registro civil*, I finally achieved success (of sorts). It was my birthday, and I considered this hard-won victory one of the best birthday gifts ever even though the results turned out to be less than expected.

Of course I anticipated being given the runaround, having become accustomed to empty promises from the petty bureaucracy in Mexico generally. This time I planned my strategies carefully in advance and was able to do some end-runs around the blocks set up to thwart me. You may wonder why people are so reluctant to grant a simple request to look at the civil register. I did too, but more on that later.

Aware that the only way to have even a ghost of a chance was to use all the palancas (levers) I could find, I asked my comadre about three weeks ago how I should go about it. She said she would speak with an uncle, a man with connections and sort of an unofficial paralegal person, well versed in the informal system of getting things done that underlies the formal system.

About a week ago this man, Tio Beto, told me he had spoken to the Secretary of the municipio government and everything was set. All I had to do was contact the Secretary, a young man I had not met. That same evening my comadre went to the Secretary's house to inquire when and where (and how much— public servants cannot be expected to do favors free). She reported that the Secretary said it was a very bad week because schools were about to reconvene and many people would be needing copies and verifications of birth certificates. He suggested meeting the next Sunday and promised to bring the registers to his home where I could look at them. Of course he would not accept any money for such a small favor (the usual courteous but insincere response), he was more than happy to accommodate, he said.

Saturday evening my comadre and I went to his house to

reconfirm the appointment for next day and set the hour. The Secretary was quite borracho but cordial (actually overly cordial, he wouldn't release my hand after our introduction). Everything was set, he said. I should come to his house at 10:00 a.m. and we would go to the city hall together to look at the registro (a change of plans already), adding something about how nice it was that I was here studying his pueblo.

On the way home my comadre said she really doubted that he would be available the next day for our appointment because it was the day of the saint's fiesta in his wife's pueblo. That was the first hint that I would probably never get to see the registro civil. Sure enough, when I went at the appointed hour he had already left hours earlier for the fiesta. Late that same night my comadre, bless her heart for such patience, went again to his house and, although still well soused from the fiesta, he suggested that I come to his house at 11:00 a.m. the next day. From this point on I was on my own because my comadre had to attend a fiesta all the following day.

By now I was pretty sure he would not be home at 11:00 a.m. but went to his house at 10:45 anyway. His wife was hosing off the sidewalk when I arrived and she informed me that he was gone to the city hall. I said I would wait if she didn't mind. She did mind and replied that waiting would be futile as he would not be back until 3:00 p.m. Not to be daunted this time, I took up a post directly across the street from his house to wait. (Otherwise he could claim he came and I was not there). At 11:45 (I was observing the time on my watch, what else is there to do on a hot street corner at noon?) a girl came by and asked if I was waiting for Pedro. I replied yes and she said that he could not come as he was very busy but I should return at 4:00 p.m. to his house. (Obviously he had been informed of my continued presence across from his house so he had to do something). I left, but returned at 3:45 p.m. and caught the Secretary still sleeping from his afternoon siesta. (He probably planned to leave the house before 4:00 p.m. to avoid me). So he had to deal with me and agreed to take me to the office which was closed for the day but for which he had the key. I copied records as fast as I could for one and a half hours after which I tipped him fifty pesos for his trouble (*His* trouble? Ha!) . . .

I did not get the statistics sought, the number of births and deaths in 1974, because the registration slips of both births and deaths had not been entered into the register but were just tossed into a box. As I thumbed through, counting births and deaths, I soon realized that the number of births was too low to be accurate and there were no death certificates for infants. Realizing that no deaths of babies under one year old for the entire year of 1974 was preposterous, I wondered about the absence of the registrations, but pretended not to notice anything unusual and continued counting and recording figures.

Causes of deaths of adults were also of great importance to my research so I paid particular attention to death certificates of adults, especially young adults. Sadly I learned that in 1974 two young people had died of tetanus, a preventable but often fatal infection, and that seven young men had died of gunshot wounds. I was not able to determine how many older people died as a result of diabetes, a very common ailment among people over thirty in San Juan, because only primary causes of death such as heart failure or stroke were listed.

Why were there no infant mortalities apparent? In some cases, no doubt, the families simply neglected to report the death, not remembering to or not perceiving the registration to be of much significance. Another answer to the mystery might have been that when a baby or small child died and the death was registered, someone could remove and destroy the birth certificate as well as the death certificate and pocket both fees. There was no proof of the accuracy of my hunch, so I kept my suspicions to myself.

I later learned two details that helped explain the Secretary's display of cooperation along with his delaying tactics: 1) The palanca, Tio Beto, was his padrino so he was obligated to go through the motions of trying to comply with his padrino's request; and 2) The Secretary had resigned his office and was serving his last few days in the job. If he had put me off only a day or two more I would have had to start again from scratch with a new secretary.

The day before Todos Santos, our household went out to the cemetery by oxcart early in the morning to clean the graves of Chica and Doña Lucia, taking buckets of fresh flowers, containers, and machetes to clear away the weeds. Going to the cemetery always made me sad, bringing back painful memories of Chica and Doña Lucia, but I was especially sad because neither of them had a proper grave marker. After seven years, the crude little wood crosses—with their initials roughly carved into them with a penknife—erected when they died, were beginning to rot away. I had wanted to erect a permanent marker for Chica ever since she died but, just beginning my teaching career and with a family partially to support, I had not been able to do so. The children of Doña Lucia were planning to order a large granite stone for her but Chica's children were still in school and had no funds. I vowed I would purchase a stone for Chica on my next trip to San Juan, no matter what.

When we returned from the cemetery we decorated the house shrine with fresh flowers and the special Todos Santos food for both Doña Lucia and Chica, whose pictures were prominently displayed along with the saints. Chica's own house had been sold by Cata who was now suffering from years of alcohol abuse and was no longer able to work.

Cata believed (and it was repeated around the pueblo) that the reason he was so sick was that Chica's spirit was haunting him. Such an accusation angered me. After all her years of suffering with a drunken husband and losing her children one after another, now people were willing to believe she was responsible for Cata's alcohol-related problems? Feli, Cata's sister with whom Chica and I had traveled to San Marcos in 1967, asked me if I thought the rumor was true. Feli and Chica had been very close friends and I thought Feli probably still felt more loyalty to Chica than to her own brother. We discussed the matter together at Feli's house one afternoon, both Feli and I citing all the favorable traits in Chica's character that would make it seem unlikely that her spirit would come back to haunt Cata. We both agreed that Chica was a soft-hearted, gentle, generous person in life and would be so in death, that it would be out of character for her to be vindictive and punishing. Feli seemed to find comfort in our talk.

In November, a week before I was to leave for home, a video team from Sweden arrived to shoot a short film for Swedish television, based on my book, *The Isthmus Zapotecs*. I had agreed in advance to act as guide and consultant for the few days they would be filming the early morning street markets, the harvesting of crops, and various home and market scenes. The fee I earned, unanticipated but much appreciated, was used to purchase a granite headstone for Chica. Doña Lucia's children ordered a similar monument for their mother. Although I was not able to see Chica's monument in place until my next return, two years later, I went home with a feeling of contentment that this last gesture of friendship, so long delayed, had been accomplished.

16

1981-1982

It was not until 1981, with a year's sabbatical leave from teaching, that I was able to once again spend a protracted period in San Juan. When I am away, communication is rudimentary at best. Although I send an occasional letter, replies are rare and delayed because informants must wait until one of their children is home and willing to write a letter for them. To get telephone calls through from the public telephone may take several days and is costly. An attempted call from this end is equally frustrating and fruitless. For these reasons, I was not sure what conditions were when I was planning the 1981-82 project.

Sandy and Ann, graduate students, accompanied me, making it almost mandatory that we rent a house for the three of us. I wrote to Chica's sister Magda, asking if we could rent her house, which had been vacant during my last visit. A letter eventually arrived confirming that we would be welcome.

In early August, the research assistants Sandy and Ann met me in Oaxaca for a final briefing, then the three of us proceeded by bus to San Juan. Bringing student assistants to San Juan was a new experience for me and no less novel for them. Although they both spoke fluent Spanish, learned during months of living in Central and South America, they had no fieldwork experience, had not formally studied anthropology, and had never been to southern Mexico. I planned to train them in field methods on the job, but was apprehensive about how they would react to San Juan. Neither Sandy nor Ann had ever lived in a small rural community with so little in the way of modern amenities.

In field briefings beforehand, I tried to be as forthright in descriptions of the pueblo and conditions as possible without painting a picture of San Juan as an earthly hell. Thinking it best to refrain from mentioning high adventures of low probability such as rabid dogs in the streets, high-noon gunfights, and earthquakes, I concentrated instead on the conditions we would have to deal with daily—precautions with food and water and means of guarding our health since we had no immunity to the local pathogens. Both young women had diligently read *The Isthmus Zapotecs* and reviewed the San Juan slides, yet I knew they would be in for a cultural jolt when we arrived. Even I, knowing full well what to expect, always have a difficult week or two adjusting to this world so far removed from the comforts of life in California.

Although I had known Magda since 1966 and over the years since Chica's death, she, her sister Faustina, and I had become close friends, neither had ever been key informants. Magda was always very busy and she was also a quiet person who preferred to listen to others rather than talk—not a characteristic sought in prospective key informants. So I was also somewhat apprehensive about living in Magda's house, situated right next door to the house in which she lived, because I was not sure how she would deal with this intrusion.

The first adjustment in our plans occurred when we learned, upon arrival, that we would be sharing the house with Magda who had sold her other home some months earlier. Sharing the house worried me, well aware of how fond we Americans are of privacy and how little it is valued in San Juan. Would Sandy and Ann prove sufficiently flexible to adjust to a lack of privacy and all the other inevitable changes of plans we would face?

Magda met us at the bus station with open arms and a wide smile. When we arrived at her house by taxi a half hour later, I noted the tremendous effort Magda had made to have everything ready and comfortable for us. Ann and Sandy were oblivious to all this and instead were struck by the garish orange and green walls, the blue and white tile floors, and the unfamiliar mixture of furnishings.

The house was spotless, the inner court swept clean. The shower room held a galvanized tub full of sparkling water for our baths, necessary because the pueblo was experiencing a chronic shortage of piped water that year. Two new hammocks hung in the corredor for our use and my old electric fan and cot had been brought over from Doña Lucia's house for me.

Magda apologized because the water she had boiled for us to drink was not cold, her old refrigerator having expired the previous week. After a supper of Magda's hearty vegetable soup and the fruit and cheese we brought from Oaxaca, we settled in for our first night in San Juan, Sandy and Ann taking the new hammocks. Magda retired to her hammock within touching distance of my cot and immediately dropped off to sleep; but sleep eluded me for hours as I mulled over the project and planned our first tasks.

The focus of our 1981-82 project was young people, ages about twelve to twenty. We hoped to identify some of the social forces within the family and community which influence this age group's gender identification and personality formation. Our sample population was to be some twenty to thirty families with one or more children of the appropriate ages. Once we had contacted the families and established rapport, the project called for conducting a series of interviews, several with each family member, recording family interactions during a series of fifteen-minute observation sessions spaced over several months, and taking group photographs of each family, both for our records and as a gift to the families in return for their cooperation. During the latter months of the project we were to administer draw-a-person and tell-a-story tests and collect a series of dreams from the young people in the study.

A letter from the field to colleagues in California describes our impressions during the first few days of settling in:

> Dear Trudy and Gang:
>
> We are here and we are lonely. No mail yet of course. I expect that it will take at least a couple of weeks to begin getting your letters and forwarded mail but we look forward to them with immense anticipation.
>
> Our first morning at Magda's house found us all awake at 4:00 a.m. There is a problem with getting water, worse than it was in previous years. Magda leaves the tap open all the time so she will know when there is water. At 4:00 a.m. the water had arrived and Magda arose and began filling buckets and carrying them to her storage tank. I must admit that none of us jumped right up to help—but we had an excuse. The water pressure was so low that it took about ten minutes to fill a single bucket so there seemed to be little point in all four of us standing about waiting for the buckets to fill.
>
> At 4:00 a.m. there is still no sign of daylight so I tried to go

back to sleep. Ha! The traffic had begun, making sleep about as probable as receiving our mail tomorrow. Two busy streets run past Magda's house, one in front and one directly in back. At 4:00 a.m. most of the traffic is oxcarts creaking past with men on their way to the fields, gentle, pleasing sounds, but it is not long before the ear-splitting, air-polluting *motos* (small motorized vehicles for hire) begin their business of carrying women and their goods to the markets and bus terminals.

At 6:00 a.m., over the noise of the motos, loud music begins. It comes from two of several public address systems scattered over the pueblo. Our house happens to pick up two of these, each from a different side. The first music is a dirge entitled "*Dios Nunca Muere*" which signals the announcements of deaths and funeral masses. Since the loudspeakers are mounted on tall poles and can be rotated for broader coverage, it is not rare for two to be booming our way at once, making different announcements simultaneously, but today we are favored with only one.

After the death announcements, market announcements boom out:

"Rosa Hernandez is selling fresh flowers from Oaxaca in the market." "Mica Lopez has *elotes* (fresh corn) for sale at her house." "Get fresh milk from Maria Gallegos at the market entrance while it lasts."

The announcements continue for a half hour or so. Then the loudspeakers go mercifully silent, a change hardly noticed since by now heavy trucks and urbanos (local buses) are moving through the streets, all with noisy unmuffled exhausts.

As we get up, bleary-eyed and groggy, Sandy remarks that the earplugs I suggested she bring are a godsend. Magda has by now gone to the market to sell some fresh corn brought in from her fields last night. We grope around the unfamiliar kitchen and finally succeed in boiling some coffee. Magda is back from the market before we finish breakfast.

Children have been pounding on the closed front window for the past half hour, shouting: "Doña Magda, sell, sell!" Magda opens up her minuscule *tienda* (store) which occupies one side of the house originally intended for a garage (this is a modern house, built to accommodate an automobile although Magda has never owned one). The children are sent by their mothers for matches, soap, kerosene, headache powders, soft drinks, and Vick's VapoRub. In between customers Magda eats a quick

> breakfast. Next, also between customers, she begins to sweep the whole living area. With interruptions, this daily task requires about two hours.
>
> That first day is typical of how all our days begin. The wind, blowing furiously since our arrival, has a renewed vigor today. The trees in the courtyard sway and swish, doors bang, and shutters rattle. Dust filters under the doors from the street like drifting snow and settles on every surface. Sweeping seems so futile. We have to wipe off a little spot on the table before beginning any paperwork and everything has to be anchored with heavy objects. By 8:00 a.m., the day's heat is already oppressive. . . .

By the end of two weeks, we were all suffering from culture shock. Ann seemed especially unhappy and depressed, several times crying privately when no mail came from home. Sandy was quite the opposite. The worse things seemed, the more she found to laugh about. Usually she could turn any situation into something humorous. If she was as depressed as Ann and I, she never let us know it.

A week or so after we began the project, Ann was running a temperature and complaining of flu-like symptoms. Soon Sandy and I were feeling the same. When Sandy's temperature rose to 104 degrees and stayed there all night we finally called a doctor. Injections of antibiotics soon had us all on the mend, relieved to find that it was non-lifethreatening dengue fever caused by the bite of a mosquito and very appropriately known as "breakbone" fever. This was a new disease since 1975, brought up from Central America with the army of refugees flooding into Mexico from El Salvador, Nicaragua, and Guatemala. The diagnosis also explained our collective mental depression, one of the symptoms of the disease.

Not much had been accomplished on the project by the end of the third week and we were all still in a sort of cultural limbo, isolated from our own culture but not even close to feeling integrated into the local community. Worse yet, we were still without mail from home.

At this juncture, Ann gave up and returned to California, increasing my apprehension about being able to carry the project to its conclusion. Yet I understood her decision. We all wanted to go home. In just the first couple of weeks we were in Magda's house we had watched five funeral processions pass the house, three carrying the caskets of small children. Could there be anything more dispiriting than the sight of black-clad mourners plodding sadly through the midday heat to the doleful accompaniment of "God Never Dies" played by an off-key band? Sandy noted sarcastically that although God may never die, in San Juan mere mortals seemed to be doing more than their share of it.

After Ann left, our resolve to get on with the project was renewed. Sandy was a happy, energetic worker who made friends quickly. Everyone liked her but she was an especial favorite with the children. We put all our energy into contacting new families, beginning interviews, and making inquiries about other prospective research families. By the end of a month we had twenty-two families with children of appropriate ages willing to cooperate with us.

We waited nearly a month for mail from home. Sandy wrote dozens of letters in her spare time, even while putting in more hours on the project than I. When the mailman finally came, the sheaf of letters were all for Sandy. Most of them she read aloud to me. One dear friend, perhaps thinking San Juan was similar to the Caribbean resort of Cancun, concluded with "You are so *lucky* to be in beautiful Mexico!" We howled with laughter at the incongruity of that expression of envy and what life was really like here. For the rest of the project, whenever things were not going as well as expected, one of us could remark "You are so lucky!" and we would dissolve into fits of laughter.

Magda and Faustina had helped me tremendously in many ways through the years since Chica's death although neither acted as key informants, a role they did not "take to." Instead they were adept at suggesting possible informants and helpers and guiding me to the sources of needed information. They were also steady founts of moral support.

In 1982 Magda was "well-off" by local standards, a widow with three grown children, all living and working at white-collar jobs in Mexico City. She owned several small parcels of land farmed by sharecroppers and leased out a cantina formerly operated by her late husband.

A gentle, compassionate person, Magda was fifty years old and, like many of her neighbors, diabetic. Faustina had a more serious form of diabetes and was insulin dependent, yet never completely able to control her blood sugar levels. It is particularly difficult for diabetics in San Juan to maintain a diet which is sufficiently low in sugar and starches. Vegetables are mostly imported from more moderate zones and can be costly. They have never been a very important part of the traditional cuisine which is based mainly on maize products, fruits, and relatively small quantities of proteins such as salt fish and salt beef. It is not uncommon for an adult to eat twenty or even thirty tortillas per day plus other maize-based foods.

Magda worked incredibly long hours. Besides taking care of and selling her crops, running the store, and curing and selling vast quantities of *ciruelas* (a native stone fruit), she had myriad social obligations, keeping up ties with her many comadres, attending weddings, funerals, novenas, and mixa gue'tu', often helping in the considerable preparations required of all these events. Occasionally she was so pressed for time that she attended some events only long enough to pay her contribution and respects, before going on to another.

Several times a month an ancient villager, bent even lower by time than the four and one-half feet of her youth, came to the house to give Magda a massage. Kind-hearted Magda would have preferred a younger, stronger curandera but continued with the frail, little Ta Na, who subsisted solely by her meager earnings.

Each time Ta Na came Magda closed the store and received her treatment on a mat on the cement floor of the store, an inconvenience caused by our presence in the rest of the house. The treatment, consisting of an alcohol rub, massage, prayers, and switching with nettles, took about half an hour after which Magda would rest for awhile wrapped in her rebozo while the old woman waited for her ten peso fee.

Rather to my surprise, I perceived that Magda was genuinely happy to have us in her home in spite of the additional work we caused. Though we tried to help by doing some of the sweeping and by helping fill the tanks and buckets when water arrived, we never arose early enough to clean the bathroom, done each day before daylight, and only once did we manage to mop out the shower area before Magda got to it.

Our project population grew to include a total of sixty-three youngsters aged twelve through twenty, a heavy research load for the two of us to handle. We hired eighteen-year-old Pancho to help after school. Pancho was known as a very good student and he caught on quickly to what we needed from him. His reliability and rapport with the project youngsters moved the research along more rapidly than we had anticipated.

A key purpose of the research was to investigate the socialization of boys, girls, and boys identified in early childhood as possibly effeminate or muxe, with the idea that we might be able to document some differences in socialization (how their families reared and trained them) among all three groups. A genetic component of the project, taking and analyzing blood samples in addition to hiring a medical doctor to do thorough physical examinations, was not funded, probably because it would have been tremendously expensive for the possibly rather small results.

The socialization part of the project proved to be flawed once we were in the field because we had no way of positively identifying boys as muxe. Family and neighbors were reluctant to label their sons and neighbors as definitely effeminate, preferring to take a "wait-and-see" attitude, and one child so identified from early childhood and known to me had, upon reaching young adulthood, suddenly shed his effeminate ways, married, and begun a family. In cases such as this, there was no way for project personnel to know if this was a permanent, lasting change, or only temporary. So we were left with a handful of effeminate boys in our sample about whom we could not predict whether their gender orientation was temporary or permanent. The only way to establish the final gender orientation of this group would be a follow-up study ten or more years later. That follow-up study is yet to be done.

Visiting our project families every few days, we inevitably became involved in events of their lives. One family was devastated when the father was killed in an automobile accident. As a result, they were unable to complete the project. Several other families had problems with alcoholic fathers which we and they managed to work around. One large family had a retarded thirteen-year-old son that especially tugged at our hearts for there were no extra family resources for him—no special classes or rehabilitation programs. We included him in our tests and interviews even though we could not use the results in our final analyses, and he returned our attention with great shows of affection. At the end of the project when he received his participant's California tee-shirt with logo, the same as his brother and two sisters, he beamed with pride.

By 1981 years of severe inflation had lowered real incomes

considerably. Some of our project teenagers waged a continual battle to stay in school, to dress decently, and to buy their school supplies while others were not able to attend school at all. Whatever their fate, their bright smiles and unflagging spirits were a source of inspiration to Sandy and me.

The years 1981-82 saw the worst conditions in San Juan in all the years known to me. Besides a steep rate of inflation, the region was in the midst of a drought of several years' duration, and the shortage of piped water had become severe and hazardous to health. The water shortage, we learned, was not caused so much by the drought as by the construction and operation of one of the largest oil refineries in the world some twenty kilometers away at the port city. This facility and the thousands of people it attracted to the Isthmus apparently had first rights to the water from the area's single water-purifying plant, leaving the native population to make out as best they could with what was left.

The most visible change in the pueblo since 1975 was the proliferation of trash in the streets. In 1966 virtually everything had been recycled, burned, or scavenged by pigs, dogs, and turkey vultures in that order. Non-biodegradables had not yet arrived. Even in 1975 street litter was not a big problem, but by 1982 the streets and hillsides were grossly littered with discarded plastic bags, waving like faded flags from bushes or swirling around the streets with every gust of wind. Broken pieces of plastic cups and spoons, the throwaways from street-purchased snacks of ice cream or gelatin, pieces of bright blue or gaudy pink plastic once used for rain and dust protection, jagged, broken bottles, and knotted plastic sacks with a plastic straw still in the knot (the new way to sell sodas) blew through the streets, or collected along curbs, finally anchored there by dirt and heavier trash. There had never been any public street-cleaning service although it was rumored that the *ayuntamiento* (municipal government) had recently purchased a garbage truck for that purpose.

Residents did not seem to notice the litter. Most people were having such a struggle just to exist that they had little energy left to "fight city hall" and insist upon a few basic public services. And what they had never had, they did not expect.

Yet the worst situation we encountered during this project period was not the poverty, water shortage, or trash but the level of open violence. For some months prior to our arrival two brothers, both in their early twenties, had been literally holding the pueblo hostage, demanding "loans" from people they thought might have some cash, commandeering taxis at gunpoint, terrorizing the populace and wantonly killing those who did not comply with their demands. San Juan had never had a genuine trained police force, only a voluntary as-needed citizenry willing to take on the job. Understandably, voluntary citizen-police were unwilling to risk their lives challenging renegades. Throughout our stay there were periodic murders. In one street incident, a sixteen-year-old girl passerby was injured and two men were killed. The night before I left San Juan for the Christmas break, the xuana was assassinated right inside the church where he had gone for sanctuary, an act so vile that it left people gasping with shock. Nobody seemed to know if drug use was involved in these despicable crimes but it was suspected. Not until May 1982, more than a year after this particular reign of terror began, were the brothers finally jailed. People were beginning to breathe a little easier, to move about with more confidence. Then, just a few days before I left for the last time, another young man was shot to death in the street by an unseen assassin.

Sandy had returned to California at Christmas to resume her classes in the spring semester. I returned to San Juan in January, after the Christmas break, to wind up the loose ends of the project. I was very concerned with conditions in San Juan and wondered what the future would bring. Everything—poverty, health, sanitation, disease, incomes—seemed worse than any other period known to me. The future looked dismal, and I returned to California with a heavy heart.

17

1990, Impressions

Except for a brief visit in 1986 I did not get back to San Juan again until November 1990 when I was able to spend four weeks renewing old acquaintances and catching up on the major events of the past few years.

Since 1982 some aspects of life seem to have improved. San Juan's serious water problems have been alleviated at least for a while by the construction of a municipal water storage facility several years ago. But the burgeoning population is evident in houses crowding up to the tops of the hills and down to the very edge of the heavily polluted trickle euphemistically still referred to as "the river." Living sites fill previously open spaces and new streets and houses have displaced the rare old trees that were formerly able to survive here and there. San Juan in 1990 gives the impression of a "boom town," bursting at the seams with people.

Many of the streets have been paved, new street lamps have been installed, a public sewer system is in place. There are more indoor toilets and showers, propane stoves, and refrigerators, and television sets are found in nearly every home. Streets are being cleaned regularly by the municipio, the market has expanded considerably, and in 1990 San Juan was officially promoted to the status of villa from its former less prestigious classification as pueblo.

The big event of 1990 was a visit from the Mexican president, who walked with his party the entire length of San Juan and spoke to an enormous and enthusiastic crowd of residents on the school grounds. This was the first visit ever by a national president in San Juan's 122-year history as a municipio. People were still excited about the event when we arrived months later and, with uncharacteristic optimism, most seemed to believe the president would keep his promises of more federal aid for the community by way of better school facilities, better roads into the remote hamlets, and a larger water storage facility for the fast-growing population.

From what we could observe in a short few weeks, health conditions have improved, more people are eligible for government health services through jobs in the nearby oil refinery, and the improved water supply and health services have decreased infant mortality from the high level we found in 1981. Families are getting smaller, most young couples planning to have no more than two or three children. Significantly, 1990 witnessed the first-ever woman member of the elected muncipio government.

Reviewing twenty-five years of intermittent fieldwork in San Juan, the most difficult aspect for me personally has been the transition required from my culture to theirs each time I return for an extended period. The contrasts are so great that, at first, everything in San Juan stands out in its wretchedness and poverty. But with time I know I will adjust and begin to perceive once again the richness and beauty of Zapotec culture which is always there just beneath the surface. For, truth to tell, the enchantment of Zapotec culture that first captured my imagination through the art and writing of Miguel Covarrubias many years ago still lives.

As I walk through the streets and hear anew the magic of the Zapotec language, see anew the colorful costumes and rituals, there is an enchantment that transcends the starkness, the raw outlines of poverty, and the dusty vistas the eye first perceives.

Women in the black of mourning, rebozos pulled over their heads, hurrying through the street in close pairs at dusk to pray at an aunt's novena, instantly transport me centuries into the past.

A special magic remains in observing the men in oxcarts coming in from the fields after sundown, the oxen's hooves making a little rhythmic tac-tac as they plod along, the squeaking axles of the carts adding their high-pitched solos to the symphony, while the driver, hat pulled low over his eyes, quietly cants his ox commands.

Fingers of excitement still run through my body when I am awakened at 2:00 a.m. to the reedy, faraway sound of the flute and the staccato tap-tap-tap of the drum as the two players of these ancient instruments pass through the streets in the eerie pre-dawn playing the age-old

Zapotec melodies that announce to the saints and the people an approaching fiesta.

La Zandunga, the people and their culture, draw me back again and again like a moth to the flame. Their sincerity, their trust, their unflagging friendship and hospitality, and the intelligence and humor they bring daily to a difficult existence continue to command my deepest respect and admiration.

"Ay, Zandunga, Zandunga, Viva La Zandunga!"

Glossary

ahijado(a) godchild
alegre happy
arroz con leche rice-milk gruel
Ay, Dios Oh, God!
Ay, Dios mio Oh my God!
ayuntamiento municipal government
baño bath, bathroom
baul trunk; carved wood wedding trunk with legs
batea shallow wood tub
borracho a drunken man or to be drunk
bruja witch
buenas noches good evening
bueno good, fine
butaca traditional low curved-back chair
cacao cocoa beans
camioneta pick-up truck
campesino farmer
cantina saloon
cantinera female owner of a cantina
cecina dried, salted beef
centenario gold coin or necklace made with it
choza reed hut
ciruela small-stone fruit; a plum
civilisados civilized persons; not barbarians
colonias subdivisions in which cities are divided
comadre ritual co-mother
comal clay griddle for cooking tortillas
compadre ritual co-father or co-parents
corredor open-roofed porch across the front of a house
cultura, de being cultured, appreciating the finer arts
curandero(a) curer
dxu stranger, foreigner (Zapotec)
elotes roasting ears (of corn)
enramada sunshade made of poles with thatched roof
en estado pregnant
evangelista Protestant missionary, especially fundamental Christian
ex-distrito a political division made up of several municipios
gringa North American woman
gringuita little American woman
gripa, la severe chest cold
hijo(a) son, daughter
huipil traditional woman's blouse
humilde humble; person of humble status
loco(a) crazy
Ma zeedu la? Zapotec greeting "You have arrived now?"
madrina godmother
marquesote ceremonial sponge cake
mayordomo fiesta sponsor
mediu xiga half gourd; a wedding rite and song
mestizo Mexican citizens speaking only Spanish
mezcal distilled alcohol similar to tequila
mira look
mixa gue'tu' death mass
mole Mexican stew with meat or fowl in a spicy sauce
mordida bribe
moto small motorized vehicle with three wheels
muertos, los the dead

municipio Mexican political division, similar to county
muxe man-woman, effeminate man
ngupi armadillo
Norte, El the north wind
novena nine-day mourning period
novio(a) fiance, fiancee
olan wide pleated lace flounce on a fiesta skirt
olla pottery jar
padrino godfather
palancas literally a crowbar or lever; someone who will act as an intermediary on one's behalf in negotiating with a third party
paleta popsicle
paletaria popsicle store
parque central plaza of a town
partera midwife
pencas palm fronds with the stems attached
pendejo an obscene word, loosely translated 'fool'
peso monetary unit
petate sleeping mat
pito y tambor flute and drum, traditional ceremonial instruments.
platero silversmith; jewelry maker
plazita small subsidiary market
posada Christmas pageantry of birth of Christ
presidente mayor
promesa vow to a saint
pues well
quien who; who's there?
rancheria hamlet
rebozo long shawl-scarf used as a head covering
redila farm truck with slat sides
registro civil civil register
rezador(a) lay prayer leader
rosario prayer session
sancudo tiny fierce-biting mosquito
santa mesa household shrine
señor gentleman
señora married woman
señorita young lady
si, tal vez yes, perhaps
siesta the hottest part of the day; sleep or rest taken during this time
solar house lot including house and outbuildings
tehuana Mestizo name for Isthmus Zapotec women
tienda store
tinajera traditional water jar
tio(a) uncle; aunt
Todos Santos All Saints' Day—November 1 and 2
totopo oven-baked, dry tortilla
tristeza sadness
urbano urban bus
vallista native of the Valley of Oaxaca
valor courage, bravery
vamonos let's go
velador night watchman
velas candles
verdad true, truth
viajero(a) traveler; traveling peddlar or market seller
viejo old man
xuana religious leader of each barrio